RED-BLOODED HR

ESSAYS ON HUMAN RESOURCES AS A FORCE FOR GOOD

LIZ RYAN

ISBN Paperback: 978-1-64184-383-6
ISBN ebook:978-1-64184-384-3

TABLE OF CONTENTS

Part One: HR Role and Mission

PART TWO: HR Policies & Practices

PART THREE: Trust & Corporate Culture

INTRODUCTION

This is a book about Human Resources as a force for good in organizations, and in the world.

I wrote these stories over the past twenty years for publications (Forbes.com, LinkedIn, the Huffington Post and others) or for the Human Workplace™ blog. Some of them are new. Almost all of them are updated from their original form.

I wrote these stories to inspire HR folks and to call out what's not working in our function - what needs to change in order for HR to reach its promise.

I wrote them to let HR people know they are not alone in seeing HR as a way to help people get more from their job than a paycheck.

As I write today, we are in the midst of a global pandemic. There has never been a time when our function was more necessary. We are operating in a different space now. The old rules for HR and the traditional HR practices no longer suffice.

To lead our organizations effectively in this unfamiliar environment, we need a new frame, or mental model, for HR.

I hope this book helps establish that frame and supports you in finding ideas and inspiration for your journey.

Liz Ryan
June 2020

PART ONE

HR ROLE AND MISSION

A NEW FRAME FOR HUMAN RESOURCES

I sat on a panel years ago at a women-in-business conference. I shared the dais with a set of very smart and accomplished leaders -- women at the top of their fields.

One panelist, a division president, was asked "What is the biggest obstacle to doing your job?"

She answered "My Human Resources department, without question. Those people are so slow and such an impediment."

I listened, down at my end of the table, with a fake smile pasted on my face.

"What's your take, Liz?" asked the moderator. I said, "My fellow panelist, like all leaders, has the HR staff she deserves."

What is an HR team if not a reflection of the CEO's vision for people and talent?

If don't like your HR people, get rid of them and get new ones. Would you blame your sales department for slowing down your agenda? Scapegoating HR is a famous, lame copout for leaders who haven't found their power.

That being said, I'm not here to sing arias about the amazingly supportive and transformational role that the vast majority of my HR brothers and sisters play in their organizations.

It's just not happening. That is the vision, to be sure, but it's not the reality at most organizations I'm familiar with. The truth is that most organizations don't take advantage of the HR talent they've got.

Over and over again, I hear the same stories of worthy HR initiatives scuttled, HR functions de-staffed and scaled back, and senior leaders tuning out on issues of culture, talent and spark. "Hey, we have a lot of business problems to solve. No time for the frilly stuff!"

The business back-to-basics agenda never seems to include noticing or acting on dysfunctional leadership teams or toxic cultures. The albatross sits on the table cracking peanut shells all over the floor, and we sit in meetings talking about whether we should require one stopover on our employees' business trips to save air travel costs, or two.

HR leaders are asked to install Talent Acquisition programs and Talent Retention programs. They spec software and install systems and build flow charts and create project plans.

But the core elements that would allow for a thoughtful examination of an employer brand or enable a more slippery recruiting process or more nimble internal communications (elements like trust, openness, collaboration, creative spark and spontaneity) are not always in the conversation. We find it hard to talk about the "soft" stuff even as HR leaders – even when it's our job to do so.

That can mean that despite an HR leader's best intentions, the process changes but the energy doesn't.

When I talk to HR leaders about The Problem, here's what they say.

"We are pulled left and right. The fact that my job and my team's function is constantly in play is a major issue. HR is the white canvas leaders can splash their hopes, dreams, fears and unresolved anxieties on. We're expected to be all things to all people."

I can relate to that one hundred percent. For twenty years as an HR leader I juggled sometimes contradictory personas, and the tension between the roles of cheerleader, strategist, coach, disciplinarian, judge, advocate and pastor never abated.

It wasn't even discussed -- we all know the frame for HR, right? HR is the group that keeps the company out of court.

HR people are the ones who write policies and enforce them.

HR are the people who are supposed to listen to you when your boss acts like a jerk.

HR people take care of benefits issues, and sign you up for training courses and issue your ID.

The HR people run the annual review process and tell your manager how much of a raise you can get.

Every manager and employee in your organization likely has a slightly different view of what HR is supposed to do. How's an HR person supposed to plow through the wall of expectations?

One minute you're handing someone a tissue as you discuss an emotional issue, and the next minute you're the prison warden holding the line on some policy violation -- or on the hook to deliver another ten percent cost reduction (without sacrificing service levels, needless to say).

The CEO's perspective is critical, of course, but here's where the white-canvas issues rears its head.

One month, your CEO's top goal is leadership team development, and the next, it's all about diversity. There's no cohesion to the action, as long as HR folks languish in the Desert of Framelessness.

We need a new frame for HR. Here's my bid.

You've got a CFO, and we'll call him Bill. Bill's job is crystal clear. Bill oversees the short- and long-term financial health of the company. That's it.

There's a vision-setting piece to the job, and an advisory and a money-cop piece and forty other pieces. There are analysts to be coddled and pension fund representatives to be soothed. There are forty other aspects to Bill's job and Bill finds a way to weave all of them together.

Bill's job is an integrated left-brain/right-brain job. If the CFO is all about the spreadsheet and can't see the bigger scope, the company is toast.

It's the same deal with your they are responsible for the short- and long-term organizational health of the business.

HR is responsible for making sure there are no obstacles between the amazing people you hired and their ability to do their jobs.

When obstacles arise, it's HR's job to tear them down.

What could those obstacles be? Here's a short list of possibilities:

- Role confusion

- Inadequate training, equipment, supplies or communication

- Fear-based management

- Contradictory priorities

- Unclear mission and/or goals

Sometimes the biggest obstacle to winning is just a lack of concern for employees in their lives outside of work. None of us has the ability to turn off our human problems and stop thinking about them just because we go to work.

When I was thrown into the job of HR manager in 1984, I was simultaneously exuberant and appalled at the number and gravity of the issues hitting my desk every day.

I'm talking about domestic violence, drug use, AIDs in its first, awful stages, mental illness, theft and physical violence. Back then, it was considered a crime to walk down Broadway in drag so we bailed employees out of jail on numerous occasions.

I spent more time on the phone with my EAP advisors than with all the company executives combined.

It was the Wild West, and every day I got lessons about one-on-one communication, teams, conflict, fear and trust. It didn't take long to notice that when managers and HR people care about employees, employees care about their work.

It's the most obvious correlation in the world, but it's neglected every day in large and small organizations.

I picked up the HR laws and the forms and the regulatory bodies in six months or so. I learned that it's more important to know where to step back and call the experts than to try to memorize employment laws myself.

HR is not a job about employment laws. It's not a systems job. It's a people job. It's a job about telling the truth and building trust on the team. It's not an easy job. You have to tell executives things they don't want to hear. You might get fired for doing that, but so what? If you care about your HR mission, you'd rather get fired than sit at your desk unable to do your job the way you know it should be done.

We need infrastructure, but infrastructure doesn't move our companies forward. If it's smart and flexible, infrastructure makes it easier for us to focus on people. If it's not, it holds us back.

If we can see the HR function through the frame "HR people make sure the environment is healthy, so the best people come here and stay here" then we take HR out of the disciplinarian role, forever.

We take them out of the Fake Fun Dispensary role, too, organizing field trips to Dave & Buster's instead of ironing whatever kinks in the energy flow are keeping the team from chugging along.

I can't imagine doing anything else in an organization. HR stuff is the only stuff that interests me, but that's because it's a people-colored view of the overall organization that helps to shift the conversation about everything from business to art to life and community.

How could that not be the most fun job around? How could any leader relegate HR to slashing travel costs and fighting unemployment claims?

What do people think companies run on, anyway? You can read the energy as soon as you walk in the door, in any retail store and any chrome-and-glass HQ.

You can feel it. You can't hide that. We are animals.

(If you've given birth or watched anyone else do it, I don't need to tell you that.)

You don't have to spend time on fake fun or fake culture if the energy is good on its own.

Our organizations are human-powered, and the employers who figure that out or always knew it will win. Their HR people already spend their time reeling in talented people and celebrating the team they've got.

Here's what they know: that any power that comes from authority ("I can make you comply!") is fake, flimsy and pathetic. It's the opposite of power. Integrity, vision, honest communication and a worldview that values people over profits gives HR leaders true power in their organizations.

Working in a talent-focused environment - where the culture celebrates people, not just on paper and in recruiting videos but every day, in the clinch - is the nirvana state for HR leaders, and I'm eternally grateful to have experienced that kind of environment.

I didn't realize, at the time, how exceptional it was. Nowadays, I preach the Minister of Culture gospel. I don't believe the Kool-Aid that tells HR people their department won't be viewed as a Serious Business Function unless they stop caring about employees.

We all deserve a new frame for HR -- employees, leaders and HR people themselves. We know the limits of left-brained, by-the-book management when living human beings are involved. We need a new theme for HR, and now's not a moment too soon to adopt one.

MANAGING THE INTANGIBLES

Dear Liz,

I'm a Human Resources Manager in a mid-sized firm. I often feel pulled between policy writing and regulatory stuff, and other projects (just listening, or creating programs) to make the environment more uplifting and engaging.

My boss is an advocate for our employees, but several of the senior leaders are more interested in uniformity than innovation and culture. I'm in the middle.

What is my responsibility to both groups and how do I navigate between them?

Thanks,
Elise

Dear Elise,

What is an HR leader's role? You could ask your boss, "Should I keep the employees happy, or be the disciplinarian and keep them in line?"

For me, an HR chief is someone who understands the business well enough (and understands people, culture and communication well enough) to create an organization where amazing people want to work.

The regulatory stuff is necessary but nowhere near sufficient. You have to do that stuff, but it can't be your focus.

You'll fill out EEO forms and teach people not to sexually harass one another. That goes without saying. Your CFO has a big regulatory task, too, but we don't say, "Our CFO's job is to keep the company out of court." Your CFO's job is to manage the short- and long-term financial health of the organization. That's easy to understand.

Your job is to manage the short- and long-term organizational health, i.e. the human health, of the organization.

There's nothing complicated about the HR mission. It doesn't require you to choose between writing the few, essential policies you need or creating a workplace where tremendous people want to be. The "defensive" tasks you must perform to stay in compliance might deserve 15 percent of your time. The intangible, critical, cultural stuff is the real meat and potatoes of an HR leader's job.

You'll look after policies and break room posters and all that jazz, but you've got higher-impact work to do. Maybe you CEO and executive team aren't on the same page regarding your culture and practices. Great! There's an opportunity for a fruitful (though potentially spicy) conversation, or an extended dialogue.

A big part of your job is to start cultural conversations when tensions arise, and to keep those conversations alive no matter what. An HR leader is doing her job when terms like "culture" and "talent" and "trust" get airtime at every leadership staff meeting (and lots of other meetings) and when the health of the organization is as high a leadership priority as a new product's expected ship date.

You could write policies all day long and benefit not one shareholder or customer. If you can get your industry's most talented folks onto your payroll and keep them, you'll have done wonders for the firm. Policy-writing and enforcement won't get you there.

You'll start by getting the leadership team singing the same cultural song. That's an HR mission you can sink your teeth into. Don't believe toxic wheeze, "If you can't measure it, you can't manage it."

The older you get, Elise, the more you'll notice that the intangible stuff is the important stuff. Only people who can't see what's right in front of them would say, "Morale? Goodwill? Trust? We can't measure those things. Better write another policy."

Best,
Liz

PUTTING "HUMAN" BACK IN HUMAN RESOURCES

It is Saturday morning, and I'm scheduling job interviews. My company got the assignment to fill an HR position for a local employer, and I'm chatting with HR job candidates about it. Some of them are all business. "Where is the company located, how many employees do they have, and what is the salary range?"

I answer their questions.

I hear a hard, clipped tone in their voices, and I think "This person has been dealt some tough blows by the universe and doesn't feel safe." Other people joke and laugh on the phone with me.

One woman asks me, "If you were me, would you love this job?" What a great question, I think.

"I did this job in another company very much like the one you're going to interview with," I said.

"It was fun and hard and overwhelming. There were policies to write and systems to put in place, and at the time, I thought that's what I was doing every day on the job. Of course, looking back, I was doing that stuff, but that wasn't the real job. The real job was to build trust on the team. It was magnificent. It's what all Human Resources people should get to do."

Human Resources -- what a concept!

People, of course, are not resources. They are warm, passionate, funny, silly, random beings with dreams and ideas and entanglements that make them awesome and complicated to be around or to work with.

What does a company need more than that?

Our client, the guy who runs the company with the HR job opening, knows about trust and fear and culture, but lots of CEOs don't. Lots of people don't feel safe enough to bring themselves to work all the way.

Some of them have brought their full, authentic, passionate selves to work before and got burned in the process.

Jobseekers are wary, and who can blame them?

For way too long, all but the most switched-on employers have treated jobseekers like dirt.

The fact that the people I'm talking with today are HR people, some of the very folks who've been charged with establishing or overseeing recruiting systems to turn people into commodities and tick marks, doesn't change a thing. They know the problem as well as anyone. They've been burned, too.

I talk to HR people about that issue all the time.

"What have you done or what are you trying to do in your company to humanize the hiring process?" I ask them. "I have no power to do that," they tell me.

"Our recruiting process is so formula-driven and mechanical there is no humanity left in it. I've talked about it at meetings until I'm blue in the face. The leadership team wants it that way."

When did we all become so powerless and so feeble against the tide of cruelty-by-automation?

When did we decide that anonymous Big-Brother-ish Black Hole recruiting systems were just the thing to bring us vibrant, switched-on and passionate people?

Or do we fear those people - is that the real issue? Do we install businesses processes right out of a dystopian novel because we're afraid that if people are too human at work, something terrible might happen?

To the clipped-tone people, I say "Ask me anything you like, about this company and this position."

Some hesitate. Do they fear it's a trap? We couldn't blame them if they do.

Some of them can't get past the rows and columns.

"What payroll vendor does this company use?" they ask.

Who the heck cares? Ask me about the culture, friend!

Ask me about the way people talk to one another in the break room. Ask me if the CEO has a heart, and not just a brain. Ask me if the CEO has a spine. Ask me about the important stuff. Maybe we are too far gone. Maybe there is no space to ask those questions of a person (like me) you don't know very, very well.

Some of the jobseekers on the phone know the human score.

"Liz," asks one woman, "Can this leadership team tell the truth to one another?"

She gets it, I think.

We'd all get it, if we could stop to remember that we're people first and working people and employees second.

Who benefits, when people shut off their creativity and spark and vulnerability to put on a suit and pretend to be robots? No one benefits -- our families and our communities suffer, our health suffers, and the whole planet suffers.

We can do better. We can bring our full selves to work.

We can be human all the way and let Staples or Office Depot supply the resources in the form of bond paper and pens and whatever else we need to get our work done.

People are anything but resources -- we could think of them as magical geese that lay golden eggs. The trick, of course, is remembering that the geese only lay those eggs when they feel valued and understood.

I tell jobseekers, "If they don't get you, they don't deserve you."

When will leadership teams get the message, stop treating their golden geese like reams of bond paper, and put the "human" back into Human Resources?

WHAT EVERY CEO NEEDS TO KNOW ABOUT HR

If you ask a CEO "What does your HR leader do?" he or she is likely to say: "You got me. I just know I need to have one."

We expect our HR execs to look after employee records, hire and train people, administer performance reviews, and see that comp and benefits practices chug along. Beyond that, the mission can get fuzzy, fast. Too many CEOs don't have a ready answer to the question "How does your HR leader help your organization compete?" nor do they have a handy list of must-do activities for an HR exec charged with boosting the organization's ability to win in its marketplace.

It's every HR chief's highest calling to make sure his or her employer has the most excited, switched-on, and capable people on the market. Here's a list of the things your HR head should be doing right now:

1. Collaborating with you and other leaders to design and communicate a vision for the company, using every communication vehicle you have.

2. Selling your company to the "talent population," in person, online, and via print and broadcast media. An HR leader should articulate the organization's culture and story, not only for recruiting purposes but to fuel all of

your activities with clients, vendors, media, and the business community.

3. Teaching employees to tell the truth at work, especially when sticky interpersonal or political wrangles crop up. (Note to CEO: This includes telling you when you stop making sense.)

4. Reinforcing a culture that emphasizes ingenuity over irrelevant, one-size-fits-all metrics.

5. Building a pipeline of qualified, energized people to fuel the company's growth—scrapping the requisition-by-requisition, transactional recruitment model.

6. Shifting the HR function away from a break/fix model ("Benefits question? Second door on the left.") to an embedded function in your business units.

7. Installing just enough HR process to meet your company's regulatory compliance needs but not so much that people are stymied or treated like children.

8. Building a culture of collaboration that fuels every important program at your company. If your HR chief isn't the advocate for people and evangelist for your culture, that's a bad sign.

9. Asking your team members every day for their input on your business, their own careers, and life in general—not via a sterile, once-a-year "employee engagement survey."

10. Replacing fear with trust at every opportunity, in policies, training sessions, management practices, and via every conversation in the place.

It's a new day in HR. Is your company on the cutting edge, or bringing up the rear?

WHY HR GETS NO RESPECT

Why is it that HR is so often the scapegoat when companies aren't getting the results they want? True, there are HR people out there who are ineffectual. But they keep their jobs at the pleasure of CEOs. Why is that?

For one thing, HR is undervalued as a function.

I have this advice for anyone who interviews for the top HR spot: When the conversation turns to your compensation, say: "I will require the same compensation as your most-highly-paid direct report." (Of course, that's only a starting point.)

As an HR leader you'll be privy to this information, so there's no fooling you. Why would a company hesitate to pay its top people officer just what its top money officer, revenue officer or product development chief is earning? Beats me -- unless the company doesn't value its people as much as it says it does.

I'm a zealot for HR, but let's be honest, many HR leaders don't function as champions for people the way the role requires.

Notwithstanding some wonderful counterexamples, the level of HR leadership in many companies falls short of what it might be, could be, and should be. Inspired and inspiring leaders aren't as often drawn to HR as one would wish -- or they're drawn to it early in their careers before being hired away for more rewarding assignments.

It's a vicious circle: HR doesn't pay what it should, so good people leave, and brilliant candidates aren't attracted to the field, so HR doesn't pay what it should, and so on.

Any CEO can snap her fingers and break that cycle, however. To do so only requires a relentless determination to find a creative, fearless, and business-savvy HR leader. Pay this person appropriately, demand that they produce results -- meaning, assemble a championship team both for now and the future -- and stand back.

With the business world changing so quickly, what competitive advantage can an organization hope to build and sustain beyond the abilities of its people?

Surely not its equipment, its methods, or even a financial advantage. You need a team that can win -- well equipped, smartly led, and highly motivated -- if you want to get ahead of the pack and stay there.

If, by contrast, it's important to you to save a few bucks on your coaching staff payroll, you had better get comfortable in the minor leagues.

Could this be another reason for the mediocrity of HR leadership in U.S. organizations -- that when things go wrong, it's always nice to have someone around to blame?

THE TOP TEN THINGS EMPLOYEES COMPLAIN TO HR ABOUT

Dear Liz,

I've just been hired into my first HR job. I'm stoked! I'm going to be the Regional HR and Recruiting Coordinator in an office with 85 people. I'll be the local HR liaison.

They haven't had an on-site HR person in this location before. My manager "Jill" told me that the employees are looking forward to having a local HR person to talk to and consult with.

You've been an HR person for a long time. What kinds of questions and issues should I study up on? What kinds of complaints do employees typically bring to HR, and how should I handle them?

Thanks Liz! You're my HR idol.

Yours,
Zoe

Dear Zoe,

Congratulations on your new job! It sounds like a great assignment.

Here are ten issues you can expect your coworkers to ask for your help with. Some of them might come across as complaints at first ("My boss is such a jerk to me" or "Why can't you people get my payroll deductions straightened out?") but like customer service interactions, they are actually great opportunities to build trust in your organization.

When you handle an employee's issue professionally and with warmth, you will quickly help to build positive energy on your team. That's the best thing an HR person can do!

Here are the top ten issues employees bring to HR (in no particular order):

1. Interpersonal challenges with their managers and/or coworkers

    (Example: "My boss is really snippy with me, and I don't know what to do about it.")

2. Payroll and benefits questions and problems

    (Example: "What are all these deductions from my paycheck? Will I get some of this money back when I file my taxes?")

3. Issues relating to their goals, objectives and performance evaluations

    (Example: "I don't think my second quarter objectives are fair. Nobody else in my department has to hit all these bars.")

4. Problems with roles, job titles and pay levels

    (Example: "I need your help talking to my manager about my job title. It doesn't match my responsibilities.")

5. Issues relating to paid and unpaid time off

    (Example: "I want to take two weeks of vacation in July and an extra week of unpaid time off. My manager said I should talk to you and find out how the company handles this kind of thing.")

6. Internal transfers and career advancement

   (Example: "Should I apply for one of these internal opportunities I see posted on the company intranet? Can you look at my resume and give me your opinion?")

7. Work/life balance questions

   (Example: "My manager schedules a department meeting every other Saturday morning. I can't make those meetings anymore. It's too disruptive to my family life. How can I let my manager know?")

8. Personal issues

   (Example: "I'm going through a terrible time with a family member who struggles with substance abuse issues. Does the company have any resources for someone in my situation?")

9. Problems with real or perceived discrimination or harassment on the job

   (Example: "One of the managers always tells me to put my hair up because he likes it that way. It's gross. I wanted you to know about it.")

10. Attendance and other policy issues

    (Example: "Everybody in my department is on salary. My boss lets some people walk into work at 9:15 and other people get in trouble for showing up at 8:45. It's not fair. Can you help?")

The hardest part of an HR job is wending your way through the tangle of relationships and power dynamics that take hold in every organization.

You will need to cultivate terrific relationships with the managers as well as the employees in your new workplace in order to broach sticky subjects with managers (like "Some of the team members in our location are concerned about arrival and departure times. They feel that we're not always consistent about our requirements around when people are supposed to get to work and when they can leave. Should we talk about that topic at one of our managers' meetings, or do you have any thoughts on that we could talk about right now?").

You'll have to tread carefully so as not to evoke a fear reaction in your managers (and you will, anyway -- it's unavoidable) while still being an advocate for your employees.

Sometimes you'll have to tell a manager they can't do what they want to do -- for instance, to put an employee on probation for no good reason, or to terminate someone just because they and the manager don't get along.

You will feel isolated at times. That's because managers have most of the power in any organization, and when you stand up for your employees, you'll be standing up against managers who want to call the shots. We can't blame them for having that view.

They were undoubtedly trained to believe that when you're a manager, you make all the rules. They don't realize that everybody has a responsibility to build a trusting culture. You're going to have to make that point home over and over.

Little by little you will build your credibility. The more that you support managers with their issues, the more they will trust you and seek out your guidance. The more they trust you, the easier it will become for you to say "Honestly Jane, in that meeting I think you lost your cool a little bit. It might be a good idea to go see Arnold one-on-one and apologize. What do you say?"

You'll become a coach to your employees and their managers, and an invaluable member of the team. It takes fortitude to hold down a job like yours, but you'll see the benefit of your hard work every day!

All the best to you,
Liz

WHY YOU CAN'T OUTSOURCE HR

Outsourcing has been all the rage for 25 years, at least. There are lots of situations where it makes sense to outsource functions.

If you're a marketing firm sending out scads of email marketing messages for your clients, you're not likely to want to manage your clients' email lists in-house.

You probably don't process your own payroll in-house, and why should you?

You may use a cleaning service to tidy up after hours. That's outsourcing, too. There's nothing inherently evil about outsourcing. There are lots of ways to get our mountains of work done, and not all of them involve W-2 employees.

But you can't outsource HR. That's like running a business in Indianapolis and using contractors in India to water the plants on the desks. HR is local. It's what's happening on the ground, in the culture and among the troops. You can't do that sort of work long-distance.

Good HR people are embedded, with at least one ear to the ground all the time. They may process vacation-time requests as part of their jobs, but their real value is in knowing where the good-and-bad-energy currents are flowing in your organization, and using that knowledge (and other skills, like sensitivity and emotional intelligence) to steer around the landmines that come with the territory whenever you work with people.

Luckily, the gulf between "process-type HR" and "people-intensive HR" duties is becoming more and more obvious every day. Much of what we used to view as standard job-description fodder for a typical HR person is now safely in the "process-type HR" arena. You can and should outsource that stuff, as long as you have a sharp HR person on staff and on premises to run interference between the troops and your outsourced-HR-process vendors. With that person (or people) in place, an employer can safely outsource at least these six programs:

- Employee Benefits processing

- 401(k) administration

- Employee Assistance Program processes

- HRIS (HR information systems) data-crunching and reporting

- Payroll

- Compensation analysis and reporting

There are other HR sub-functions that are safe (and may be wise) to delegate to partners outside your company's walls. You can see what our outsourceable functions have in common: they have to do with data, with numbers and cells in spreadsheets.

That data and those reports inform and help you manage the movement of human energy, which is the principal thing that fuels your business. As long as you've got someone on hand and on site who can make a call to your benefits administrator to advocate for an employee when a health claim gets denied unfairly, there's no problem outsourcing the left-brain side of the HR assignment.

(If you haven't empowered your local HR person to advocate for your employees with your third-party vendors, you have a problem. If people aren't being paid correctly or their benefits aren't being processed the right way, your HR person will have no juice or credibility to talk with employees about anything else.)

We could almost stop calling the left-brain, quantitative sub-functions listed above (payroll, benefits, HRIS and so on) HR functions at all. At best, they are HR operations tasks. The real HR work is the part that can't be outsourced, because it happens in the moment and on the ground. Here is a list of 30 situations where an immediate, local, well-informed HR presence is irreplaceable:

1. Your purchasing manager is furious about an unfortunate incident with a vendor and wants to fire or discipline the employee who goofed up.

2. A mailroom employee had a crisis at home and isn't sure when he can come back to work.

3. Two managers have a jurisdictional dispute and need some help sorting out where the lines of responsibility fall.

4. The CEO is concerned that your Marketing VP may not be right for the job.

5. The circulation department manager, who is doing a lot of hiring, seems to hire only white female candidates.

6. There's unrest in accounting, where an unpopular supervisor was recently promoted to assistant manager and is way too comfortable telling staff members how to do their jobs (in detail).

7. Two of your directors can't agree on when the facility will be open vs. closed over the holidays.

8. An IT employee announces that they are transitioning from female to male and would like the company's support.

9. The new-hire sales ninja is causing tension on the salesforce and their coworkers are up in arms.

10. Your most experienced inventory person says he's planning to retire a year from now; you have no one remotely qualified to replace him.

11. Your front-desk receptionist was arrested for DUI over the weekend and is serving 30 days in the county jail.

12. A pregnant mom on your staff asks you, "How come there's no lactation room here?"

13. The employees like your new health plan in general, but the much-higher deductible is causing a lot of unhappiness.

14. Through conversation you realize that virtually no one understands the sales compensation plan.

15. An employee's mom is seriously ill, and the employee needs help managing through the crisis.

16. The company is growing too fast for internal infrastructure to keep up with sales growth.

17. Your New Employee Orientation program is so dated you are embarrassed to deliver it.

18. The CEO's wife is driving the CEO's administrative assistant over the edge.

19. The CEO himself, while a wonderful person, is tone-deaf in the employee communications department.

20. Two of your top tech folks are talking about taking their favorite idea and making a startup out of it. They'd like your company's investment; there's a question as to whether their idea is actually your company's idea.

21. There was an incident between two young marketing folks at a conference in Las Vegas, and nobody's talking about it back in the office. (Except that everyone is talking about it.)

22. Somebody on the staff has a problem with appropriate discussion of religious beliefs.

23. There are glaring mismatches between the levels of incentive stock options some employees have received and the contributions they have made vis-a-vis others.

24. Morale is terrible.

25. No one understands the company's strategic plan.

26. There was a workplace violence incidence in the same office park, and your organization has yet to address that issue.

27. There's a rumor one of your managers is too free with sexist comments.

28. An employee is very unhappy with their recent internal interview process.

29. Your recruiting process is frustrating to candidates and employees who refer them for open positions.

30. You work among humans. Bottom of Form

This list describes 30 of the 10 million ways that people-focused HR makes a difference. Your local, irreplaceable, embedded HR person may know how to move forms around, but his or her real value is in solving problems involving actual people.

There's all the difference in the world between designing a sales-comp plan in the abstract and problem-solving in a real organization, with salespeople who care a lot about their quotas and how they get paid.

That's what HR people do — they dig into a situation to see what's not working, have lots of conversations about it and do lots of listening, and then work with the people around them to craft a solution that straightens out whatever is causing a kink in the energy flow. They take away roadblocks to focus and creativity. They build community. They spread pixie dust around.

You can't outsource that!

It's foolish to try.

Lots of companies have viewed HR as mostly an administrative function up to now. The administrative parts of HR are the ones that you can outsource without losing sleep.

The person-to-person, Minister of Culture duties are the ones you must keep in-house. If you don't have a person fulfilling that role in your organization, you can use the money you save on outsourcing the processes to hire one.

Real HR work is human. That's why it's fun, and why it's as strategic as your five-year plan, if not more so.

TEN THINGS YOU DESERVE FROM YOUR JOB -- BESIDES A PAYCHECK

Dear Liz,

I started my job a year ago. I have been waiting for the job to improve -- to become more rewarding and interesting.

At first my manager "Allie" told me that she was moving me into the position slowly because I was new, and she wanted to make sure I learned the procedures perfectly.

After three months I knew my duties cold and Allie said, "I'm going to introduce you to new responsibilities, but I'm going to do it gradually."

That has never happened. Every time I inquire about learning something new or stepping outside my boring and entry-level job description, Allie makes an excuse.

Allie is afraid to give people responsibility because she wants to make all the decisions. You can see it on her face and in her body when she's anxious because a lowly employee (me or one of my co-workers) uses their brain and has a good idea.

Allie is insecure. After one year I've been permitted to attend exactly two meetings. Neither of them included any managers besides

Allie, because Allie does not let me or my teammates interact with other managers -- ever.

She doesn't want anyone to know us or know what we're capable of.

I need more from my job than to carry out the same routine tasks day after day, with no training and no reinforcement for my work.

I'm getting ready to launch a job search but I'm wondering: what should I be looking for in a new job?

Thanks Liz!

Yours,
Corinne

Dear Corinne,

Each of us gets to decide what's important in a new job, and that's just as it should be.

Here are 10 things I believe that every working person deserves from a job -- besides a paycheck:

1. A pleasant, safe and comfortable working environment free of physical dangers (including mold in the ventilation system or other building-related hazards) and free of harassment, bullying or discrimination. That workplace could be at home (depending on the job) or almost anywhere. Wherever you work, you deserve the right equipment, tools, training, communication and support to do your job.

2. A trusting environment in which employees can speak their minds without fear of punishment.

3. A supportive environment for teamwork, collaboration and innovation.

4. Acknowledgment for an employee's hard work, and honesty in communication.

5. Competent and ethical leadership and supervision.

6. Fair treatment, wages and management policies.

7. The opportunity to grow professionally and personally.

8. An employer/employee relationship that gives equal weight to both parties' needs.

9. Reasonable employee benefits including paid vacation, sick and personal time.

10. Respect for their lives outside of work.

Here in the U.S., employment laws do not require employers to provide all of these things to employees. Employers have to follow laws concerning wages and hours, and they have to provide a safe workplace. Most of the items on the list above aren't addressed by employment laws.

You deserve more than merely what employment laws require. You will find some workplaces where the management philosophy is "We've got a job opening for you -- take it or leave it!"

You will find other workplaces where most or all of the good things on our list are part of the package. That's the kind of job to shoot for!

It could be in any industry and any size employer. Small companies do not have a monopoly on talent-aware cultures and big companies are not necessarily worse places to work than small companies are. You have to go on a job interview and see for yourself!

You have to ask lots of questions and keep your spidey sense on full alert. Apart from your job interviews themselves, pay close attention to your communication with the employer's representatives (via email, text and voice calls) during your interviewing process.

If you stay tuned in, you will be able to tell whether your prospective employer and your prospective boss deserve your talents or not.

You already have a job. You don't need just any job to replace the one you've got.

You need and deserve a new job that will value you as a contributor -- not tolerate you as a carbon-based production unit. Be willing to slam doors on the wrong opportunities -- that's the best way to bring the right ones in!

All the best,
Liz

WHY HR CAN'T INNOVATE

The so-called talent shortage is a major topic at human resources and recruiting conferences.

It is strange that even though every hiring manager knows that the sharpest candidates don't stay on the market long, corporate recruiting processes don't change. They don't get nimbler or faster. They don't get less burdensome or bureaucratic. You'd think that employers hungry for talent would innovate, making their recruiting processes easier and more human.

The worst thing about the crisis in recruiting is the notion that the best-qualified candidate for a job is the one willing to climb over the most piles of broken glass to get the job.

No wonder hiring managers take a person who is more likely to be the most-compliant—rather than the most-talented—candidate. We could call this person the Last Candidate Standing.

The whole encrusted recruiting process (not to mention unfriendly, robotic auto-responders and the unending stream of honesty tests, writing tests, and other recruiting hurdles) makes it easy for organizations to hire drones, and it makes it hard for them to hire the brilliant and complex people they need to solve their problems.

Here is a list of six ways broken recruiting processes work together to keep great people out of organizations while pulling in not the most talented but the most docile candidates.

- Compose job descriptions that list all the tasks the new hire will perform plus a long list of Essential Requirements the ideal candidate must possess. (We all know they aren't essential at all.) Don't talk about the mission; make the job description as bland as possible. Don't sell the candidate on the job. Why would they need to be sold?

- Write a job description that insults the reader from the start, using such language as: "Only applicants with "Blah, Blah, Blah" will be considered." Make sure the tone is such that readers know your company rules the roost—and that he or she will be lucky to get a word in reply if they take the time to apply for the job.

- Send interested applicants to a horrendously slow-moving and tedious recruiting website and require them to spend two hours or so filling out forms and uploading documents. For extra points, blow up the application two or three times while candidates are working on submissions.

- Throw screening tests and extra requirements at candidates throughout the process, just to keep them guessing.

- Take weeks or months to get back to people to schedule job interviews. At the interviews, keep them waiting in the lobby, ask idiotic questions like "What is your greatest weakness?" and get offended when they inquire about the actual state of the team, the salary level or the company's commitment to the planet and/or diversity.

- Finally, leave candidates in the dark while you prepare low-ball offers, and then send the offers via e-mail with a message that says "We must receive your acceptance within 12 hours, or this offer will be null and void."

The off-putting legalese is the final touch that will come close to guaranteeing that any job-seeker with an ounce of backbone or self-esteem will flee, leaving you free to hire the most docile and compliant person, aka the Last Candidate Standing.

The sad part is that it's so easy to improve your recruiting process and give your company a massive boost in competitive advantage. You can get there in small steps. What are you waiting for?

THE CERTIFICATION RACKET

There's a brouhaha in the HR world. The long-established professional HR certification bestowed by the certification partner of the largest HR association is in transition. The HR association has snipped its connection to the certifying body and will be creating its own certification. Where does that leave already-certified HR people? Will their old certification be worthless now?

The tumult brings to mind the Dr. Seuss story "The Sneetches." In that story, yellow Sneetches (who live on beaches) are living a pleasant beach existence until their calm is shattered by the arrival of a canny monkey, Sylvester McMonkey McBean, who offers to put stars on each Sneetch's belly for just two dollars apiece. This way the Star-Bellied Sneetches will be able to tell themselves and their Star-Bellied brethren from the un-star-bellied Sneetches.

As soon as every Sneetch has coughed up the two bucks to get a star on its belly, of course, McBean convinces the Sneetches that the new style is to have NO star! Back into the machine go all the Sneetches, and McBean makes a fortune on the frenzy to stay on the right side of the star-belly fashion line.

The HR community looks a lot like the Sneetch community right now. Plenty of HR leaders are asking "Do I need to go through the whole certification process again? Is my old certification still worth what I paid for it?" They are seeing the limits of the externally conferred certification paradigm. This is why I call the setup (and this column) The Certification Racket.

What is a racket? It's a con, a shell game. Professional education is fine by me. I think continuous learning is great. It's the 'starbelly' aspect of certification that bothers me. Somebody creates a certification in anything -- project management, HR leadership, database administration or anything else you can think of -- and they work to get it accepted. If they're successful, hiring managers and HR folks start including the certification as a necessary requirement for new position openings.

These HR folks and hiring managers may not have earned the certification themselves. They may have no idea what the certification even measures. No problem! If a certification becomes popular, everybody's going to start demanding it in their new hires, and of course, that's what the certification companies want.

A certification is a racket if the only value of the certification is to become 'qualified' for jobs that only require the certification because it's popular. Speaking from experience, I think any HR certification falls squarely into that zone. I was an HR leader for decades. Let me tell you what an HR person needs:

- To be a good listener
- To be able to connect the dots between people, processes and organizational culture
- To tell the truth about sticky subjects
- To be able to write and speak in a human and easily understandable way

That's it. If you know that Griggs v. Duke Power was one of the landmark cases in the early days of equal employment opportunity, so what? If you know what the Halo Effect is and how it might affect a manager's appraisal of a well-liked employee, so what? Any certification for a human function like HR that relies on taking a written test and answering the questions correctly is pointless. How could answering questions correctly possibly make you a better HR person?

I don't blame people for seeking certifications. They have no choice when those certifications are listed in half the job ads they see!

That's one reason we teach jobseekers not to apply through the standard portal, to ignore the Black Hole recruiting sites and reach their hiring managers directly.

People whose resumes are full of certifications have bought into a broken system. The certification world is only as sturdy as the faith that other people put in it.

When a certification loses steam as the HR certification is in danger of doing, we see through the frayed fabric into the heart of the machine. Certification without real-life experience is not a way to evaluate people for employment, period.

If I taught you thousands of facts about HR and then sent you out into the world, how would your knowledge of those facts in the abstract possibly equip you for the real-world challenges you will face? Certification-by-fact is a ridiculous notion, because if all I wanted was to get the most common thousand facts into circulation at corporations and institutions, I'd hire a techie to write a phone app and give it away for free.

There'd be no point in tying up millions of person-hours studying for and taking tests. If all we want to do is move facts around, that's easy and costs almost nothing. People armed with facts are not better project managers, better HR people or better anything. Certifications that enrich their creators and make hiring authorities feel really discerning and choosy are a pure racket, and unworthy of smart and nimble people.

If you want to follow a thought leader whose ideas speak to you, then follow. Take guidance wherever you can find it and listen to your own heart and brain above all. The HR flap reminds us that all wisdom comes from other people. Why would we ever believe that there's one way to do HR and that some personality-free, philosophy-less certifying body would have a lock on that one way?

This is our folly, and our opportunity to remind ourselves where learning really lies. No certification will make you smarter or more strategic, nor will any degree or trophy conferred by someone else. Step out of the certification-collection zone and listen to the people and situations around you.

Watch your flame grow, then!

TEN REASONS EVERYBODY HATES HR

I became an HR person in 1984. I managed Customer Service and Operations before I was put into my first HR job by my boss, John Brady, who told me when I came back from vacation, "You're the HR Manager now." I said, "What?"

I was sad to leave my team in the Order Processing department. We had a fantastic crew and we had fun. I was sad because I thought that being an HR person meant that I wouldn't be able to talk to our customers or sales reps anymore. I loved our customers and our salespeople. We laughed and joked on the phone all day.

John said, "Go ahead and talk to whoever you want." He got me to see a bigger vision for HR, before I had spent 10 minutes in the HR department. John said, "The purpose of HR is to make this organization an awesome place to work and to make sure we don't do anything stupid." I liked that vision. I dug right in.

I didn't realize during most of my 50,000 years as an HR leader that many or most people hate HR. They fear HR people. I didn't know that at the time. I thought my job was to be the den mother and pixie-dust-distributor in our company. I didn't realize that many HR leaders who would like to be den mothers or dads and pixie-dust-distributors aren't allowed to do that.

In many organizations the role of HR is to keep the company out of court. The role of HR is to keep the company from getting sued -- by its own employees! Can you imagine a sadder or less inspiring reason to come to work? Does your CFO stand up at the executives' meeting and say, "It was a good month -- none of our customers or vendors sued us!" Of course not.

It's a given that your customers and vendors won't sue you unless a truly terrible and unlikely set of events take place. You'll have plenty of warning if that event sequence begins. It works exactly the same way in HR, but fearful leaders and fearful HR people see imaginary ready-to-sue-them employees around every corner!

I never spent two seconds during my eons in HR worrying about getting sued by my fellow employees. We were having too much fun to think about suing one another. If somebody was unhappy, a manager or another employee or an HR person would hear about it. Then we could figure it out and get past it.

Waves of good and bad energy circulate in every organization.

All we have to do is pay attention to them. It easy to do that -- we almost can't help it! We are humans. Humans are animals. We know when the energy around is positive and when it's negative. We need to start telling the truth about that.

Here are ten reasons people hate HR. None of them is inevitable or built into the HR function. Not one of them is an intractable problem. If you are an HR person, you can start to address this issue today. You can step out of the traditional HR box and bring yourself fully to your role, with your humor, your warmth and your quirks. You can do HR your own way!

10 Reasons People Hate HR

- HR people seem to take the company's side in any interaction, never the employee's side.

- HR people seem to want to get employees in trouble for tiny infractions.

- HR people are not viewed as trustworthy, even though they say, "Tell me what's on your mind!"

- HR people stand idly by while incompetent and abusive supervisors get promoted and mistreat employees.

- HR people often "know HR" but don't know anything about the business they work for, or about how to talk with and listen to employees.

- HR people often spout policy instead of actively getting involved to remove roadblocks their employees face.

- HR people are seen as political and more concerned with their own place in the company's pecking order than with the welfare of the team.

- HR people talk more about policies, benefits and other announcements than they talk about culture, fear, trust, conflict or any of the million human issues that arise in every organization.

- HR people often have trouble seeing the "human side" of any issue, from a time-off request to a variation in a pay-grade or a hiring issue, focusing instead on keeping every process uniform and exception-free.

- HR people, who can be Ministers of Culture in their organizations, are too often seen as culture-killers instead!

What can a leader do if his or her organization's HR function is not living up to its potential? The first step is to look in the mirror! Too many executives lead HR, if they lead it at all, through fear rather than trust. They focus on keeping payroll costs down and keeping "employee issues" to a minimum, instead of setting ambitious goals and then hiring brilliant people to help achieve them -- and letting those brilliant people do their jobs.

The world is changing too fast for stuck-in-the-mud organizations to survive. HR has a big job to do, but it won't happen until HR people and their colleagues come together to acknowledge and celebrate the critical cultural role that empowered and switched-on HR people fill.

PART TWO

HR POLICIES & PRACTICES

THE TRUTH ABOUT BEST PRACTICES

For decades in the business world I've been hearing about Best Practices.

They're not Best Practices. They're just somebody else's used practices, passed on from one boring, uncreative company to the next. Best Practices are the business equivalent of a forty-year-old fruitcake.

Fear-based managers love to talk about Best Practices. It's their way of saying, "Somebody else already figured out the right way to do this."

Is there a "right" way? Every organization is different.

best way to do something is the way that makes sense in the moment and in context. All the information that would influence the answer to the question "What is our best option here?" is found in the situation itself.

We can't pretend that porting old, moldy practices from one company to another and one context to the next is smart, or even responsible.

If we trusted the people we so painstakingly hire to do the jobs they do, we'd let them have a lot more latitude and say-so than they get. That's our fear showing itself. "No, no, no! We've already set that procedure. Don't you dare change it!"

Maybe the landscape has changed since somebody else's Best Practice was installed. It is the nature of physical systems, after all, to change and keep changing.

It's only in the grey, stodgy and stultified business and institutional worlds that we pretend that things aren't changing all around us. We pretend that we can sit around a conference table and write a Best Practice, print it into manuals and call it good. We delude ourselves that that's a great solution to any problem.

What if we shared our vision for our organization and shared some pointers for folks who aren't sure how to proceed, and let our talented and brilliant employees figure out the best solution based on the facts at hand?

Of course, the facts at hand can include anything from a customer or co-worker's tone of voice to the date (nearer or further from month-end, for instance) to the urgency of the other issues on your desk or your To Do list.

We hire adults, so why not let them behave as adults do, and make decisions based on what they perceive in the ecosystem? That's how our species survived this long. We didn't make it here from the veldt and the savannah by repeating other people's rules and hard-as-rock fruitcake practices.

I was a corporate HR leader for eons. I think I heard three good ideas from other companies during that time. The first one I recall was the idea of paying employees to bring in their friends for job openings in our company. We glommed onto that in a heartbeat.

The second good idea I picked up at an HR conference was the notion of allowing interested employees to be part of the interviewing team for job openings in their department. That was a big hit, too.

The third good idea I took away from an HR gathering was the idea of giving every new parent in our company a car seat for the baby. The rest of the good stuff we did, we came up with on our own. It was our company and our culture -- of course we're going to do things in the best way for us!

We told our salaried employees "Take off the personal time you need. We're not counting your days off. Get your work done, of course, and let us know when you won't be at work on a given day." Twenty years, and no problems with the policy we called the Come to Work Policy.

We gave our employees latitude when it came to inter-departmental transfers. Why involve a department manager in a possible intra-company move unless it's actually going to happen? There is no equivalent barrier when an employee decides to job hunt outside the company.

We told our employees that after one year in their first job in the company, they were free-range chickens. They could apply for any job they wanted to in the company. HR would set up the interview, and if it didn't go anywhere, their current manager didn't have to bother him- or herself about it. They simply wouldn't know, unless the employee chose to tell them.

We didn't have starting times or ending times of the workday for salaried employees. That's why they're on salary in the first place! We had no problems. Practices devised for the actual community of people you've assembled are always the best practices.

We consult with employers now. We say "Here are some things you could try. Here are some ideas. They're only Best Practices if they work for you." The differences between organizations are more significant than the similarities. Every culture is different. If we go from job to job installing the same tired set of Best Practices in every one, why even hire humans? You could get a machine to do that.

Teams of people energized around a goal always come up with the best solutions. They'll blow your mind with their solutions if you trust them to feel the energy and pay attention to the landscape. If you don't trust them, they can always pick up some boilerplate Best Practices and subject your employees to those. Is that the best thing for your customers, or for your team?

That depends. How human do you want your organization to be, and how responsive to the environment you're in? The choice, of course, is yours.

You could force ancient fruitcakes on your team or let them loose in the kitchen to bake up something miraculous -- a magical concoction of their own.

SEVEN EASY WAYS TO LISTEN TO YOUR TEAM (WITHOUT TAKING A SURVEY)

Dear Liz,

I manage a team of order processors and expediters for my company. Our team has a good time and gets a lot of work done.

My boss, the Director of Operations for our company, knows my views on our annual employee survey process.

He told me "I know surveying the employees is not the best answer because the survey results are not specific enough to be useful.

"When things are going well in a department, the employees ignore the survey request and then we end up having to berate them via email to complete the survey. It's a bad process, but I don't see an alternative."

Can you please suggest some alternatives to our unpopular annual survey process? We want to take the pulse of our employees rather than just patting ourselves on the back as a management team by saying "We have an 81% employee engagement level so we must be doing things right!"

What do you suggest?

Thanks Liz!

Yours,
Shane

Dear Shane,

Hats off to you and your boss! A good rule of thumb when you're evaluating a management or HR practice is to ask, "Is the practice I am considering one that promotes trust, or is it a practice that rests on fear?"

"Confidential" employee surveys (sometimes called Employee Engagement Surveys) rest on fear. That's why employees are allowed (and sometimes compelled) to complete them confidentially!

As soon you tell the employees "Don't be afraid -- you can complete the survey confidentially!" you have already failed.

Can you imagine confidentially surveying your family members to get their opinions on the state of your household? A survey could not help you if there weren't enough trust in your own family to have honest conversations.

Every parent's aspiration is to build trust and warmth in their family.

If things got so bad in your household that people were not talking -- for instance, if your children stopped talking to you -- you would deal with that issue instead of accepting it as a feature of human nature.

You wouldn't tell yourself "My kids won't talk to me. They don't trust me. That's okay! I'll send them a confidential survey to complete."

Many dying, dead and ripe-for-extinction HR and management processes are rooted in fear. 360-degree feedback systems, like confidential employee surveys, presume that confidentiality is needed for honesty to come out.

Forced or stack ranking of employees is obviously a fear-based process because it ties an employee's future to their ranking among their peers, throwing your team into dog-eat-dog cage competition when you (and your customers) need them to support one another!

Performance reviews and the larger notion of performance management rest on fear. The idea behind performance reviews is that the manager sits on a high perch and peers down at each employee to grade their performance -- the way kids are graded in school.

We don't treat entrepreneurs like children -- but we treat employees that way.

No one makes the vendor who waters your office plants sit down once a year to hear what they did well and what they did badly.

If your firm no longer requires the plant-tender's services, then they don't renew their contract. Smart vendors get their contract-renewal conversations out of the way months in advance so that they have time to find new clients for the new year if they need to.

Why doesn't employment work the same way?

We treat employees like children because it is part of the mindset surrounding employment as an institution. The parent/child dynamic is baked into the institution, and that's why we still have processes like Progressive Discipline, 360-degree feedback and "confidential" employee surveys in place.

Luckily you can ditch the "confidential" employee survey and replace it with simpler, timelier and more human alternatives. It is easy to listen to your team, but you have to shift your mindset away from mechanical processes (like surveys) and toward human interactions to get there.

SEVEN WAYS TO LISTEN TO YOUR TEAM (WITHOUT TAKING A SURVEY)

1. Help every manager get in the habit of stopping by each of their teammates' desks or workstations two or three times a week if not more often. Your purpose in those short visits is not to 'supervise' your teammate but rather to build trust. Ask each person "How are you doing? Do you need anything from me?" When you get an answer to that question, make the employee's need a priority. That's how you will begin to build trust on your team -- and begin to hear more and more about how people feel and what they're thinking. When folks work remotely, you'll do this via technology, where it works just as well (as long as you only listen and offer support – resisting the urge to micro-manage!).

2. Make every staff meeting a feedback opportunity. Put it on the meeting agenda: Views or State of the Team or Topics That Need Airtime. Get in the habit of getting off the agenda you had in mind and talking about what your team wants to discuss. Even if it's only ten minutes per week, this activity will build trust and let you know about

topics that need discussion before they become urgent. Of course, you have to honor and respect what you hear, even if you don't like it.

3. Make your "open door policy" a reality that employees can believe in. Reserve two or three time slots a week when you can chat with your employees about whatever they want to address. The more you listen, the more people will trust you. You cannot lead a team by giving directions all the time. You have to be open to feedback, ask for it, acknowledge and thank employees for it when you get it, and act on it when appropriate.

4. Organize a department lunch or virtual gathering with lunches paid for once a month or as often as your budget will allow (since your budget is paying for lunch) and use those lunches not to talk about your business metrics and plans but to talk about the team itself. Ask your teammates "How are we doing with communication on our team -- and communication with me? What can we change and improve? What hot issues should we address today?"

5. Get your entire team together physically or virtually for a Town Hall Meeting with your top leader. Ask employees to submit questions in advance so the person leading the Town Hall meeting can prepare answers. If your team's trust level is high enough, people will also ask impromptu questions during the Town Hall Meeting. Don't be afraid to gather your employees for fear they will ambush you. It is your openness to hear from them that will build trust on your team.

6. Beyond department staff meetings and Town Hall meetings, every gathering in your company is an opportunity for trust-building. When you deliver a training workshop, get the participants talking with folks from other departments. Build in an activity that encourages your

workshop participants to apply whatever they're learning to their own department and to share ideas with people from other groups. When you build trusting relationships across functions, the whole team benefits -- but community-building has not often been seen as the business imperative it is!

7. Establish at least three back channels employees can use when something is going wrong or concerning them. Good back channels include a confidential telephone hotline, a general email address that employees can use to report problems, a virtual Suggestion Box, a designated HR person to contact with sensitive and/or urgent issues and the understanding that any manager -- not just your own -- can listen to and help resolve employee issues. An annual survey is the worst imaginable back channel, not only because it is so infrequent but also because to maintain confidentiality and thus protect themselves employees have to report problems so generally and generically that it's almost impossible to act on their reports.

As leadership and HR teams evolve and realize that building trust and free-flowing communication in their organization is the single best way to achieve their business goals, more and more of them are adopting trust-building activities.

They are smart leaders because their organizations will find it easier to recruit, keep great people excited, and move faster and more nimbly than their competitors!

All the best,
Liz

HERE'S WHERE TO STICK YOUR PERFORMANCE IMPROVEMENT PLAN

Dear Liz,

I work for a successful boutique consulting firm. I'm a Project Manager. I've worked here for almost five years. I established myself here a long time ago. The Managing Director loves my work. All the managers know me.

I've worked for three different Directors in the company and they were all great to work for.

Six months ago, there was a company reorganization.

I was moved to a new team. I understand the logic behind the re-organization, but it was abrupt. The integration has not been smooth. My role stayed the same in general, but it was reduced in scope because the projects I'm responsible for are not close to the company's core expertise or relevant to our most important clients.

I mentioned to my new manager "Nora" that I can take on more responsibility. It was a good faith gesture, but she reacted badly.

Nora immediately got huffy. She said, "You will prove yourself in this new capacity, and then you'll get bigger projects. I decide who works on what -- not you."

I was stunned by Nora's reaction. I didn't ask for a pay raise or a title change.

Nora is very insecure about her authority. Since I became her team member, she has looked for opportunities to throw up roadblocks and limit my effectiveness.

I have worked for managers who ignored me. That didn't bother me. Nora doesn't ignore me. She deliberately undermines me. She talks behind my back. She pulls projects out from under me. I have never run into this type of managerial sabotage before.

Nora is hyper competitive. She is the least popular manager in our organization.

I confidentially asked a friend of mine in HR why Nora is so negative and back-biting, especially toward me. My friend said, "Nora is afraid of you. You have more credibility around here than she does. She doesn't want you to succeed."

"Okay, fine," I said, "but then why is she allowed to supervise me? Don't the leaders care if I leave?"

My friend said, "Of course they care. Nobody wants you to leave, but the leaders don't want to get involved. They figure you can deal with Nora better than most of our Project Managers could. They're hoping they get lucky somehow, like maybe Nora will quit. Her own manager is afraid of her. Nobody wants to confront her."

My warm feelings toward the company disappeared in that instant. I started job hunting the following weekend. When my friend in HR told me that the company's leaders weren't going to do anything to improve my situation or get Nora off my back, I knew it was time to go.

I wasn't fast enough, I guess. A week after my conversation with my HR friend, I got pulled into HR for a disciplinary meeting. I got an email message twenty minutes before my meeting in HR was scheduled to start.

There are 75 employees in our office. It's not a massive corporation, but I got hauled into HR in the most formal, insulting way you can imagine. Nora was already there when I arrived. The HR Manager was there. They both looked very solemn.

The HR Manager said, "We need to talk with you about your Performance Improvement Plan." I'm a five-year employee with a great track record and great relationships all over the company, and I got ambushed in HR with a Performance Improvement Plan.

I wasn't having it. I said, "Let's be honest. Nora and I do not work well together. We don't mesh. That doesn't make either of us right or wrong, but it suggests we should not be working together as closely as we do. This is not a situation that calls for a Performance Improvement Plan. It's a situation that calls for an adult discussion about where Nora and I can each be most effective.

"My work is exceptional and everyone in this room knows that. I'm not going to sit through some ridiculous disciplinary process trumped up to justify Nora getting rid of me. If you want to talk like adults about a severance package, then we can have that conversation."

I was full of righteous indignation. I didn't care what Nora or the HR Manager thought about my opinion, but I wasn't going to sit there and suffer through the Performance Improvement Plan charade.

Both Nora and the HR Manager looked like they were going to faint. The HR Manager wavered. She wasn't ready to commit to Nora's made-up Performance Improvement Plan. She said, "It's good we're having this conversation." That's when I knew I was not going to get fired -- at least not that day.

After our meeting I couldn't focus. I was still in shock. I texted our CEO and said, "Please call me when you have time." The CEO is my boss's boss's boss but like I said, I've been here for a long time and I know the CEO well. He called me about an hour later. I stepped outside to take his call.

I explained the situation to my CEO. I stayed calm. I said, "It's your company. It's your decision what to do. I don't have to stay in the company but I'm not willing to go out under a cloud of poor performance, as you can understand."

He did understand He called my VP, who is Nora's boss. We all met the following morning: me, Nora, our VP and the CEO.

Nora's "case" against me melted into a pile of nothing at that meeting, but I still felt bruised. Why was there so little oversight while Nora was tormenting me?

Nora made a fool of herself in the meeting with the VP and the CEO. All she could say was, "Gennifer isn't committed to my team." She couldn't point to one error, oversight or failure on my part.

I was honest. I had no reason to hold back. I told the CEO and my VP that it wasn't just Nora -- the leadership culture and communication in the company has gone downhill dramatically in the company, during the time we were growing fast and adding layers. The CEO and the VP had very little to say. The evidence was right in front of them.

They both said nice things about me and nice things about Nora, as you would expect.

The next day my VP offered me a newly created position reporting to a different Director. I said I would take the job on a six-month contract. I was still reeling from being dragged into HR to sign a Performance Improvement Plan.

Now I'm working for my new boss on one of the most interesting assignments I've had here, but I'm still job hunting. This experience woke me up. If I had had one drop less credibility with our CEO or one drop less confidence, I would be on probation right now and scrambling to keep my toxic ex-boss Nora happy. I would be in a desperate situation, trying to find a new job before I got fired.

Most people will not go over their boss's head. It seems like a risky strategy. In my case it was the only thing to do but I understand why most people wouldn't dream of contacting their boss's boss directly.

You might be wondering what happened to Nora and whether she's getting more leadership guidance now. My friend in HR tipped me off. She said, "It's one of those things where Nora will probably be gone from the company in three months, but they're taking it slowly."

I don't believe Nora is save-able as a manager but then again, I've never managed people. It took me making a ruckus to get my CEO and VP to notice that they had someone petty, vindictive and in over her head in a leadership role. Why were they so asleep at the wheel?

I understand the need to be fair and coach people who are struggling but I really have to wonder whether Nora's remaining employees are also being coached and supported while they suffer under Nora's management style every day. I doubt it!

It really hit me that just because someone is a VP or a CEO, it doesn't make them brave. It doesn't make them a person who can always stand up for and act on their values.

It's a good learning experience, but painful. Thanks for your support of all of us, Liz!

Yours,
Gennifer

Dear Gennifer,

Pat yourself on the back for finding your voice and your backbone when it mattered! I'm glad you are job-hunting.

Your CEO and VP did the right thing that day in the meeting with you and Nora but they are struggling to maintain trust in the organization as it grows, and you are smart to take the next exit ramp.

Fear is rampant in corporations, start-ups, not-for-profit agencies and pretty much every workplace. The healthiest organizations talk about fear and insecurity. The majority of them don't.

Your story is a great reminder that working people have more influence than they think they do. When you know you are right (and righteous) you can speak up. I wish more people would do it! We understand why they don't. Fear is a powerful emotion.

Every time you step through that invisible membrane between fear and trust, you grow your muscles, but you also do something even more important. You inspire someone else. You show them how to stand up for yourself.

Performance Improvement Plans are part of the toxic machinery that keeps fear in place and keeps working people walking on eggshells when they should be standing in their power, accomplishing great things. Performance Improvement Plans should have gone extinct in the Mad Men era. There are plenty of other companies that can use your brilliance. We are rooting for you as you go out and find one!

All the best,
Liz

10 HR POLICIES YOUR COMPETITORS WILL THANK YOU FOR

Sometimes I wonder what CEOs think happens to people who leave their company in disgust.

Where do they think those employees go? They go straight into the arms of your competitors.

They work for your competitor and they call their friends at your company and say "Hey, the grass is a lot greener over here!"

I know because I loved to hire employees who had friends back at their old workplaces. We gave them bonuses to bring their friends to work with us, but they told us that they would have recruited their friends even without the bonus. A great working environment is your best recruiting pitch, and of course a great work atmosphere makes your company more profitable, too.

There's no reason to have awful, talent-repelling HR policies in place, and I say that as a former Fortune 500 HR chief. Any policy that smacks of Big Brother-ism or that sends the message "We treat our employees like children, or inmates" cannot help your company in any way, but it certainly help your competitors.

At U.S. Robotics we had a tough time competing against Cisco Systems when we paid people $125K for jobs that Cisco paid $200K for. We lost some excellent employees, but our products didn't have the sky-high margins that Cisco's products had. We had to be creative to keep people on board, and so we got creative.

USR had always been a great place to work, but we spent more and more of our time and energy talking about the environment, opportunities for advancement and the general tone and tenor of our shop. That is what you have to do if you want to keep great people on board.

Above all, you can't hem in your employees with old-fashioned rules and policies that insult the talented adults who work alongside you. Here are 10 talent-repelling HR policies that have no function in a modern workplace.

If you have any of these awful policies still hanging around, start talking about it at your organization.

Sound the alarm! These policies will drive your best employees straight to your competitors. Get rid of them now!

No References Policy

If you don't let your managers give references for former employees because you don't trust your managers not to slime people, why are they managers in the first place? Your former colleagues deserve references from their managers, period. It is unethical and unprofessional to withhold them.

No Casual Time Off Policy

Salaried employees don't stop working when they walk out the door. Don't treat them like chain gang members by refusing to let them leave work an hour early or arrive an hour late when they have personal business. We entered the Knowledge Economy at least twenty-five years ago. Step into it!

We're Stealing Your Miles Policy

Employees whose tushes sit in airline seats deserve the frequent flyer miles their trips accrue. Those hard-earned miles belong to your employees, not to you. If you can't afford to fly people to places you need them to be, shut the doors and sell the assets - you are done.

Prove Your Grandma Died Policy

If you require your employees to provide written proof of a family member's death to receive a few days' paid time off, you have no business holding a leadership position. If you don't trust your employees, do you trust yourself to hire people you trust? One would have to conclude that you don't. Learn to trust yourself and other people or get out of management.

Primary School Dress Code Policy

The more specific a dress code is, the more uptight and weenified your culture is. The best dress code policy is the one that says, "Dress professionally for work, and if you're on the fence about a particular outfit, err on the side of caution and wear something else."

Bell Curve Performance Review Policy

If you believe that your managers must have hired and kept only twenty percent awesome people and twenty percent above-average performers, meaning that sixty percent of the people on your payroll shouldn't even be there, you will make it true. If you don't trust your managers to evaluate people honestly there are folks who will happily buy your company from you and run it like a business.

The first step is to kill the bell curve and the next step, of course, is to ditch performance reviews altogether.

Restrictive Internal Transfer Policy

An employee can quit at any time and go work for your fiercest competitor. They don't need your approval to do that. Why would you let an employee's current manager decide when and whether the employee can transfer into a new position internally? Requiring a manager's approval on internal employee moves is a great way to drive your best people out the door.

You Quit, You Suck Policy

If you are so freaked out about an employee leaving you to go to a competitor that you'd walk your formerly-trusted employee out the door the minute s/he gives notice, you are a fearful weenie with a serious problem. I have said a friendly good-bye with hugs and sometimes tears to many people who went to my company's competitors, and not one of them took anything confidential with them or screwed us in any way.

Why would they, since we were all friends? When you mistrust your employees and show it, expect to be mistrusted back.

Stack Ranking Policy

If there is stack ranking (sometimes called forced ranking) going on anywhere in your organization, get rid of the practice this week! It is a heinous anti-leadership process that has no business benefit whatsoever and does tremendous harm to the fabric of your organization. People are not pieces of lumber to be stacked up and compared to one another. Teamwork is something you have to earn, and you won't do that by pitting team members against one another.

No-Moonlighting Policy, Forced Arbitration Policy, & Non-Compete Policies that aren't really necessary

Just say no to these insulting practices that never helped a company get or keep talent.

HOW AT-WILL EMPLOYMENT HURTS BUSINESS

Several years ago I wrote a story about the rights that employees could have at work if companies felt like raising the talent-snagging-and-retaining bar to hang onto their best employees.

You should have seen the messages hitting my inbox after the story ran. If you can picture a person screaming hysterically with spittle flying out the corners of his mouth and then picture those words arriving in an email message, you've got the picture.

I mostly heard from lawyers who represent employers in employment-law matters.

"Employees have too many rights already!" shrieked my correspondents. "Your list of 'rights' would create a nightmare scenario for employers and the courts."

Their messages bring up a good question: why are the courts involved in day-to-day employment issues? It's so that most aggrieved employees will give up easily. They won't sue. They won't file a claim, because it's a pain in the neck to do so.

That's not how employment matters work in most of the industrialized world. You don't have to go to court to get relief when your employer fails to honor your employment contract. In other industrialized countries, employees have contracts! They can't be fired on a whim for no reason, the way they can in the US.

A fundamental principle underlying the employment relationship in the U.S. is captured in a doctrine known as Employment at Will. It says that just as an employee can fly the coop at any moment, so can an employer decide that a given employee's services are no longer needed. It doesn't matter how long the employee has held the job.

As long as the reason for termination isn't discriminatory (that is, you can't be fired for being Black or Presbyterian, or disabled or female or over 40) an employer can dismiss any employee it pleases at any moment. The doctrine of Employment at Will speaks loudly, even in companies that don't go about tossing talent out the door for bad reasons. Every employee knows that any given day on the job could be his or her last.

You can get fired for being a Cubs fan, or for preferring Elvis to the Beatles or vice versa. In lots of places, you can be fired for being gay. You can be fired for being Republican or for being shorter than the boss would like their VP of Sales to be. You can be fired for your Mississippi accent, or for saying "good morning" in a way that bugs your manager. As an employee at any level, you have no effective job security at all.

Of course, you can quit your job at any time as well. The unexpected departure of a key employee is a hardship for an employer, but the unexpected disappearance of your job on an ordinary Tuesday afternoon is a personal and/or a family crisis. It may not be easy to replace an employee who leaves an employer for greener pastures, but at least there are other employees around to fill in the gap.

When you lose your job, you lose your income, your professional identity and (for most of us) much of your self-confidence and self-esteem. Not many working people would throw those things away lightly.

That's why the Employment at Will doctrine hurts American businesses -- because it keeps working people focused on behaviors that will preserve their employment status, at the expense of airing ideas and issues whose open discussion would be in the best interests of their employers.

If you worked for a company that made it clear that people won't be terminated for speaking their minds, for telling the truth about hard-to-discuss, sticky issues, or for trivial reasons unrelated to their performance, what could you expect? You would expect people to speak more freely and to debate their managers more forcefully.

In that scenario, the level of control managers wield would shrink a bit, but the level of thoughtful discourse about business decisions would skyrocket. If people weren't so worried about being kicked to the curb for telling the executives what they don't want to hear, they'd speak more forcefully and give their employers better advice. Employees and managers could spend less time on political research ("What's Barry likely to say if I support Suzanne's idea?") and more time on making the business run profitably.

Employers set the tone for their adherence to and reliance on the Employment at Will doctrine. Mature leaders make it clear through their actions that vocal, well-meaning employees won't be silenced through banishment. A contrarian employee might be told, "That conversation is really over, Garrett. We're going with the clamshell design, and we know you hate it. We have to move on" but s/he wouldn't feel threatened in the process. Those "dissent is welcome" employers win in three ways:

- They get to keep the brilliant, sometimes prickly, eyes-open and provocative employees whose good ideas fuel their product development, marketing and operational efforts every day.

- They get to hear what their workers are really thinking, because the veiled threat "If we don't like what you have to say, you're history" has disappeared.

- They get to learn how to manage through trust and conversation, versus fear and control.

Giving up control is seldom fun or easy, but it teaches us higher-level skills – as parents, or as leaders. When I worked for a company that tolerated a higher-than-usual level of internal debate, many meetings were stormy.

We'd get mad at one another and fume and bluster, but there was never a thought of firing anyone for his views. That would have been crazy, as our mindset was "His views? They're extreme – most of them aren't practical – but there's always something useful in his rants." If we want our employees to tell us the truth, all we have to do is prove to them that we want it enough to hear it without bringing the hammer down.

The Employment at Will doctrine is a great example of control that hurts us more than it helps. How many great ideas do we miss out on because employees don't trust us to rise above petty reactions ("Who is he to have that idea? That isn't even a Marketing issue. What is that employee trying to pull?") when their suggestions threaten the hierarchical status quo?

How many important decisions do we flub because the specter of Employment at Will keeps the yes-men-and-women around us nodding their heads and saying "Sure, Boss, whatever you want" when their hearts and minds are screaming "Oh my God, you are an idiot"? Sometimes you have to give up control to gain control. If employers could trust themselves enough to give up the control embedded in the Employment at Will standard, imagine the innovation and creativity they could tap.

Every employee needs a contract guaranteeing their employment for a defined period of time or indefinitely, unless they do something that warrants their termination. We are far past the point when Employment at Will was healthy or productive, either for employees or their employers.

THE HORRIBLE TRUTH ABOUT 360-DEGREE FEEDBACK

I was the Energizer Bunny of HR for ages. I was all over the latest trends. My teammates and I were busy bees.

I am sorry to say that I jumped on and implemented some godawful HR ideas back then but at least I had the horse sense to ditch the worst HR fads quickly.

I should have nuked annual performance reviews and I'll bet I could have talked my righteous leadership team into that idea in about eight minutes. I feel bad about my failure to name the elephant in that case.

The silver lining is that my cognitive dissonance over the HR weenie methods I left in place as a sitting HR leader impelled me (together with many other influences) to launch the Human Workplace™ movement to reinvent work for people.

Even sharp and forward-looking people who see clearly how broken our traditional top-down, fear-based, command-and-control organizations are struggle with the pros and cons of 360-degree feedback.

I didn't even struggle: I heard that 360-degree feedback was the latest HR trend and I was all over it.

I brought 360-degree feedback systems into our company in a big way. It makes me queasy to write those words because 360-degree feedback is as evil and anti-human a mindset and methodology as you could find anywhere in the fearful, bureaucratic workplace.

It just doesn't look that way from the outside.

"Look!" we say. "One teammate can help another. Honest, compassionate feedback from your supportive co-workers, supervisors and others will give you the specific guidance you need to understand how you're viewed by others."

You can wrap 360-degree feedback in pretty colors and pawn it off as almost a self-help project. That's bunk. 360-degree feedback is the grown-up version of a horrible game played in middle schools.

We had the game in my middle school in the seventies and my son has it in his middle school right now. We called the game Slap Book -- I've heard it called Slam Book, too.

A Slam Book is a plain spiral notebook on which a kid has written the name of each middle-schooler on a separate page. Kids pass the book around and write comments about their fellow students.

Middle schoolers are not known for their tact or ability to empathize with others.

They are still growing those muscles. Kids write vicious things on the pages associated with each of their teammates. Of course, when one of your schoolmates hands you the Slam Book, you flip immediately to your own page to read what the other kids wrote about you.

Needless to say, the comments are anonymous. Depending when the Slam Book gets passed to you by another kid, each page will have just a few or dozens of comments scrawled on it in middle-school script:

"Fat."

"Ugly."

"Smart but a dork."

"Pretty but mean."

"Her sister is ugly."

The kids fill up these books with comments and everybody ends up feeling badly.

360-degree feedback teaches working people that the way to support and help one another is to complete anonymous, secret feedback forms for your colleagues and tell them what they need to improve, in your opinion.

You can tell them whatever you want without having to step up and own your comments or own the relationship between you and the person you are 'coaching' through your feedback.

360-degree feedback systems shred the fabric of trust in an organization. We can teach people to share honest, compassionate feedback with all the context that useful feedback requires, like this:

Sally: Jonas, can I ask you a quick question?

Jonas: Sure!

Sally: Last week, at the staff meeting -- I'm sure that something I said hit you wrong or I said it badly or something -- I just wanted to ask you about that because I could see on your face that you weren't thrilled. I wonder if you remember?

Jonas: Oh - well, we were talking about product numbering and you said "Vince mentioned that he wants the product numbers to correspond to the kit numbers" but there are a number of problems with that approach. I didn't want to dig into that then and there, at the staff meeting.

Sally: Okay. Did you talk to Vince about that by chance?

Jonas: No. You know how it is with Vince. You have to have a crystal-clear 30-second conclusion that Vince can give a thumbs-up or thumbs-down to. I wanted to talk to you first so we could figure out the best plan and then go see Vince together, but I forgot about it right after the meeting. Thanks for reminding me.

Sally: No problem. Want to set up a time to get together and talk about the product numbering scheme?

Jonas: Great. Can I make a suggestion? You did a great job laying out the problem we're having with the product numbering system --

Sally: But it could have been an even better job. Okay. Lay it on me!

Jonas: Listen, you know I'm a big fan of yours, Sally. Here's the thing. When you mentioned Vince wanting the product numbers to correspond to the kit numbers -

Sally: You're thinking I should have kept quiet about that.

Jonas: I'm not sure there was any advantage to bringing up Vince. It wasn't really a studied opinion that Vince offered. I remember the conversation -- Vince came into our product meeting just as it was wrapping up, last month. He said, "We already have kit numbers -- do we really need a whole separate product numbering scheme?" He was asking a question. He was also exhausted. He had just gotten off a flight from Norway - remember?

Sally: So, I kind of stacked the deck in the staff meeting, you mean, by bringing Vince into it.

Jonas: In a way. If we conclude that we really do need a separate product numbering system, now our whole department may feel like "Vince already weighed in on that topic!" I'm not sure that's an accurate assessment. When we have to chance to look at the question with some altitude, we may well decide that tying the product numbers to the kit numbers will hurt us in several ways.

Sally: Oh, geez. Okay. That's good feedback, Jonas. I appreciate it. I really appreciate your coaching. I say stuff like that sometimes -- I guess I get nervous and I feel like I have to throw Vince's name in there when I'm not sure of the right answer.

Jonas: Everybody feels that way sometimes. You're still new in this job. In a way, throwing Vince's name into the conversation weakens your point. It says, "Don't listen to me -- I just invoked our boss's boss's name -- pay attention to his opinion, instead of mine!" I want to help you be seen as even more credible than you are in our company, and you are already credible, especially being so new.

Sally: You're the best, Jonas. You should be a manager.

Jonas: Not my cup of tea but thank you. You can talk to me about anything on the job that perplexes you. You could talk to Marjorie if I'm not around. That's what the rest of us are here for.

We don't need to fill out sneaky forms behind one another's backs and hand them in to a Central Scrutinizer who will spit out useless, garbled, context-free "feedback" in the form of ratings (Excellent, Good, Fair and Sucktastic) for your hapless co-worker to take home and stew over.

360-degree feedback offers fearful people the perfect opportunity to take potshots at their colleagues and sends the false message that mechanized, inhuman batches of disconnected 'feedback' are just as good as human, contextual, supportive coaching but every living being knows that isn't true.

Middle school can be brutal, but the flip side is that once we're out of middle school, we never have to do it over again. Let's not bring middle school into our offices, factories and sales floors. We are adults now. We can look one another in the eye and tell one another the truth, the way adults have done since our species began.

Questions and Answers

What about anonymous feedback to report a lousy manager? Isn't that a good reason to keep using 360-degree feedback systems?

No! There are many other, less 'batch-oriented' ways to get continuous and instant feedback to various people in your organization if something bad or inappropriate happens between you and your manager.

Good organizations are like wheels of Swiss cheese. They have channels and tunnels running up, down and across their organizations. It is easy to establish confidential feedback systems that don't require employees to fill out long forms and submit them.

Especially these days, when personal technology is ubiquitous, it is easy to connect any employee or contractor with the people who need to hear from him or her.

My employees don't have the kind of relationship Jonas has with Sally in your example. How could I encourage better teamwork?

You can create an environment where those kinds of supportive team member relationships will naturally occur and thrive. The first step is to get rid of excess yardsticks and pointless rules that hem employees in and make them fearful. You can role model a better way of communicating, too.

When everyone is worried about staying on the boss's good side or worried about getting a bad performance review, naturally they will tend to pick at one another and compare their performance to their peers.'

That is horrible for teamwork and for whatever good results your company or institution was hoping to achieve. Your first step as a leader is to remove the barriers to trust that are keeping your employees eyeing one another suspiciously instead of supporting one another.

HOW JUNK SCIENCE SET
HR BACK FIFTY YEARS

Nearly every young person has had the same experience I've had --
the experience of hearing older people talking about serious topics
you don't understand and assuming they know what they're talking
about, then later finding out they don't.

That's what happened to me as a young HR person. I got into
HR in 1984, when I was twenty-four years old and the Cubs lost to
the Padres three games to two in the National League Championship
Series.

Junk science in HR was a new thing back then. It was all the
rage. I guzzled down the toxic lemonade. It was the nineteen-eighties,
and made-up correlations and pasteboard analytics ruled the day in
HR. It took me a while to figure out that almost everything I was
learning at HR seminars was nonsense.

One of the hot new trends back then was three-sixty-degree feedback, a crock of culture-destroying junk science that said that you'll
get better, more honest feedback when you turn your co-workers
into Secret Shoppers spilling the beans on their own co-workers.

Who knows how many millions of dollars employers have
invested in three-sixty-degree feedback programs that shred the
trust level on their teams and keep people guessing about which of
their co-workers they can trust and which they can't?

Three-sixty-degree feedback systems are a perfect example of junk science in HR. There is nothing scientific about secretly polling people about the supposed strengths and weaknesses of their teammates. If you value trust on the team, you'll teach people to talk honestly to one another.

If you delude yourself that anonymous feedback from the sky that comes without context and without any regard for the relationship behind the feedback is awesome, then you'll think that 360-degree feedback schemes are the bee's knees.

HR people and the leaders who employ them have a habit of going gaga over any idiotic tool that comes along, as long as it seems 'scientific.'

If there are numbers involved, if there's an algorithm in the mix and if we can score people on their results, we're enraptured. Whether we're screening jobseekers, collecting feedback on our teammates or evaluating someone's performance, the more numbers and rating scales we can employ, the happier we are!

High-trust teams don't use pseudo-scientific tools and performance metrics. They don't need them! If you can't tell whether someone is pulling his or her weight without measuring their output beyond what your five senses tell you, you have problems that no HR tool can help you solve.

You have a leadership problem in that case. You have a leader -- or more than one -- who can't manage their way out of a paper bag.

There is nothing remotely scientific about the junk-science tools that make hundreds of millions of dollars for the vendors that peddle them and cause misery to employees around the world, but a lot of corporate and institutional HR people don't trouble themselves about that.

They run with the herd.

Traditional employee evaluation systems are junk science in action. Thank God I worked with engineers and technical people.

Technical folks ask the right questions. I wasn't in HR for more than a year or two before a software engineer co-worker of mine asked me the critical question about performance evaluation.

He pulled a loose thread on a sweater and got me thinking. Pretty soon the whole sweater unraveled. Here's our conversation went:

Software Guy: So, Liz, every year our company evaluates every employee and tells them that they did a good job on some things and a bad job on other things -- right?

Me: Yep.

Software Guy: So, what's the yardstick? What are people being measured on?

Me: Their goals, of course!

Software Guy: But what's the yardstick? How do we determine how well someone did at their job, whether they have goals or not?

Are we measuring an employee's performance relative to the best employee in the company -- if we could even determine that, and keeping in mind that almost everyone here has a different job description -- or against what we believe is each person's potential -- if we could hope to know that?

If someone gets "straight As" on their performance review, does that mean they did the job as well as any human being could, or that they worked at the level of their highest potential, filtered through the subjective lens of their manager's opinion?

Me: I have a headache.

All the Software Guy was telling me was that individual performance evaluation systems are a crock of junk science. We try to be analytical and precise in our Human Capital Management strategies, but we fool ourselves. We try to employ particle logic when we're dealing with waves.

What are the waves made of? They're made of human passion and commitment -- to one another, to the goal, to the mission - to lots of important things. We bring junk science into a wholly organic system and too often, we destroy teamwork and trust in the process.

All our beloved junk science does is to frustrate our employees and slow them down. Our rating systems and analytics take our teammates' focus away from the one thing that could help us win -- namely the good energy on the team that sustains us and moves us forward.

We hire people based on junk science when we assign personality traits and characteristics to a job opening and then test the applicants to see who possesses the personality traits we think we need.

Who is a manager to say that a job "requires" this or that personality trait? There is no substance to that assertion at all. Yet we install fake-scientific screening tools and call ourselves responsible recruiters. That's a travesty and a disservice to our shareholders.

Junk science is rampant in the HR department. Its use represents irresponsible overreaching that costs our companies money and drives talent away from our organizations.

Myers-Briggs, the Enneagram and DiSC profiles, as fun to chit-chat about and compare notes on as they are, are parlor games. They don't tell us who is best suited to perform which job.

We might as well say "I need a vegan Capricorn in this job" as to designate the Myers-Briggs profile for the job candidate that we believe can perform best in the role, yet many companies do just that.

Over the past fifty years we've talked ourselves into the belief that algorithms can tell us more about the people around us -- and even about ourselves -- than our own experience and a million years of human evolution can.

That's where we go wrong!

I grew up as an HR person in small companies that got big. When you work closely with a small group of people, you get to know them well. You trust them and they trust you.

It is foolish to disrupt the energy by inserting junk science into the middle of it. Science is great for calculating the distance between stars and solving physical, mechanical, biological and chemical problems among many other applications.

We lie to ourselves when we pretend that made-up rubrics and formulas can help us build great teams or achieve anything momentous. Junk science has set the HR function back at least a half-century.

We should be far past our juvenile obsession with calculating, counting and sorting. We should we experts at removing the Energy

Blockers that get in our way, but we can't even see them. We are drunk on junk science and can't give it up.

We have prayed to the wrong god for way too long. It's time for every leader and HR person to remember that human beings operate by different rules than mechanical parts.

We have intuition and insight, whimsy and flashes of brilliance that machines aren't capable of. Those human abilities don't reduce down to measurable particles, so we ignore them or pretend they don't matter.

We won't measure our way to great teams or big visions. We won't analyze our way to our goals.

We won't inspire any result worth achieving by applying algorithms to our teammates and their activities. We are smart enough to see that. It's time to get rid of the junk science that powers nearly every HR department and blocks the forward motion of our teams.

Work is populated by people. It's a new year, and a great time to stop pretending that we can junk-science our way to success. We can stop pretending there's a magic algorithm that will help us win.

The more junk science we pile on the HR heap, the more out of touch and irrelevant the HR department becomes.

The first word in Human Resources is "human." Can we stop pretending that we can reduce human behavior and human potential to an $X + Y = Z$ equation and tell the truth about what powers our results? If we can do that, there is hope for us yet.

WHY 'FORCED' JOB RANKINGS DON'T WORK

Ten million years ago, when Ronald Reagan was President and gigantic reptiles ruled the earth, I was a young HR person in training. During those days, I went to countless management-training seminars, and heard this mantra over and over: "Management is comprised of four activities. The four activities of Management are planning, forecasting, budgeting, and controlling."

Don't laugh! This was solemn wisdom, back in the eighties.

Over the years, we stopped talking about management, and started talking about leadership. There was no more emphasis on forecasting, budgeting, and so on (all of which, if you think about it, are activities that can easily be done by non-management folks), replaced by talk of leadership topics like creating a vision, inspiring greatness, and motivating teams. I couldn't have been happier to live through the management-to-leadership transition, as I'd been more interested in the "people" side of management than the budgeting/forecasting stuff, which put me right to sleep.

After a dozen or so years of reading every leadership book I could get my hands on, from <u>The One Minute Manager</u> to <u>The Leadership Challenge</u> to <u>Good to Great</u> and zillions of others, earning a master's degree in Communication Studies and attending more leadership training sessions than I care to remember, I thought I knew a thing or two about inspired leadership.

Not only that, but my role heading HR for a growing company gave me some influence on the leadership practices in the company, and the ways by which new leaders were trained. At my boss's urging, I launched a local networking group for HR leaders in our city (Chicago), and began to share best practices with my peers.

An Anti-Teamwork System

Now, imagine my shock when HR leader after HR leader told me that his or her company had adopted a forced ranking system as part of its performance-management framework, and shared the details of how their companies deployed the forced ranking technique.

If you're not familiar with it, forced ranking is a scheme that companies use to compare their employees to one another, by ranking one person in the department as best, another person as second best, and so on.

Everyone gets a place in the ranking: some poor soul, of course, is last, someone else is second to last, and so on. Some companies lop off the bottom 10%; most companies who use forced ranking attach pay increases to an employee's place on the list.

I was incredulous. "You talk about teamwork, a winning culture, and everyone pulling together, but when it matters most you turn abruptly to the philosophy of every man for himself?" I asked. "How can you credibly preach 'the whole is greater than the sum of its parts' when, once a year, the whole team is elbowing one another for the top spots on the list?"

Employees Are Individuals

Also, this approach made no sense to me because all my leadership training had taught me that people are complex organisms, with unique skills and talents. How could you possibly say, "You're best" or "You're worst"? Is there even be a single dimension ("Good workerliness?") by which employees can so easily be rated? One person is great at project planning but would collapse in a tense customer-facing situation. Another person, a lady nearing retirement, performs only two tasks from her cube in the corner, but the company would be sunk without her. You get the idea.

Ranking people is not like organizing screwdrivers in your toolbox by size. Andre might be a good worker, but teamed with Rajeev, he becomes a great one.

The leadership talent that inspired you to put Tiffany, Gretchen, and Thuy together on the product-launch team has made all of them stronger contributors and brought great benefits to the company. What could be the benefit of ignoring these interdependencies, and lining your team up in a zero-sum game of "Who's Better Than Whom?"

I thought the idea of forced ranking systems was horrifying in the abstract. It was even worse when my schoolmate Susan came back to class after a break one day and said, "Listen to this. I just got a voicemail from my manager, congratulating me on being slotted into 17th place in our team of 42 employees." Hearing that made me literally sick to my stomach. How is that kind of a message useful performance feedback?

Look at the Larger Purpose

If you think about American leadership lore, you'll quickly see that we recognize the value of teams and promoting shared goals. People become greater than they were when they began the quest—whether it's in a World War II buddy movie, A League of Their Own, The Magnificent Seven, or any number of other "teamwork" films you could name. There are countless stories of how people become greater than they were before they began their quest by fitting their talents into the team's larger purpose.

These teamwork stories show us the skinny, wisecracking kid from Brooklyn; the grizzled, cynical veteran; the outsider; and the rest of the gang finding a way to work together and achieve tremendous things. How does forced ranking fit into that picture?

It doesn't.

Good managers—and I trust that's the only kind of manager you're hiring and the only kind you hope to be—evaluate people on their own merits and abilities, asking and expecting each one to surmount obstacles and become a better contributor year over year.

Good managers also handle performance problems without benefit of a forced ranking system that compels them to identify their biggest loser and other bottom-of-the-pack players.

They don't need artificial, forced mechanisms to promote excellence and deal with problems, and they certainly don't need a corporate forced ranking process to stymie their efforts at building teamwork and collaboration every day of the year—no exceptions.

THE THREE MOST EXPENSIVE BUSINESS SCAMS

Getting scammed is the worst. Not only do you waste money when you're the victim of a scammer, but you feel like an idiot for letting it happen to you, too.

We hear all the time about scams in private life, from people peddling fake investment schemes to teams of guys who drive up to your house and offer to repave your driveway for a low-low price, then do a horrible job at it and take off to scam the next person.

Right in our neighborhood we had a Ponzi schemer who is now serving twenty years in prison. I always drove by his house when he was living here and thought "Dang! That guy has expensive cars in his garage." He used to leave the garage doors up. Now we know how my neighbor funded his car purchases --- with other people's money!

We hear about consumer scams, but there are far bigger scams at work in the business world. Businesses waste hundreds of millions of dollars every year on just the top three business scams alone. These scams are insanely expensive, they waste time and frustrate people, but we allow ourselves to be scammed over and over again, year after year.

Why? We haven't figured out their scam nature yet, although it's staring us in the face.

A scam is an offer to do something worthwhile and valuable. The offer is a scam when it doesn't give us, the buyers, what we paid for. A business scam is an idea that is sold to us under the banner "This will solve your problem," but these three time-and-money-sucking business scams don't do that.

They waste time and money, deplete the focus and good energy of our teams and destroy the cultural fabric of our organizations, which is trust. Do you have any of these three expensive business scams playing out in your organization? Most large companies are infected with all three of them!

Most Expensive Business Scam Number One: Performance Management

Performance management is a dogma that rises to the level of religious devotion for its adherents, but it's based on nothing. Performance management is a set of tedious, insulting and time-wasting practices that measure the output of individual employees down to the smallest measurable activity.

You can buy software to measure the speed of your employees' individual keystrokes and quantify the number of minutes and seconds they spend on every email message and every website they visit. These are fear-based measurement tools for managers who don't know how to lead and organizations that don't understand people.

Performance management has a cult of devotees who believe that the way to win at business is to slice and dice each employee's output into minute parts tied to pre-set, measurable goals.

These fearful non-managers have forgotten that people only achieve great things when they get excited, and when they have the latitude to act on that excitement.

Even organizations who are not members of the cult use annual performance reviews to measure their employees' performance, because they've always been told that a responsible employer should do that.

As a former Fortune 500 HR leader I can tell you with assurance that annual performance reviews do nothing to help your organization succeed and are quite effective at holding you back.

They waste an astonishing number of people-hours, suck the energy away from your actual business and create internal strife. That is why more and more organizations are ditching their annual performance reviews.

There is no basis for the idea that when individual employees are measured down to the nibs, the team's performance improves. Measurement itself is a distraction from the main events: building great products and serving customers. Right now is a great time to ditch the expensive, time-wasting Performance Management tools and systems and focus on trust and forward momentum instead.

Most Expensive Business Scam Number Two: Employee Engagement

There is now a big industry built around the idea that external intervention is the key to improving a made-up metric called Employee Engagement. It's a scam! We can invent fake constructs all day long, but talking about them doesn't make them real.

People connect to their work when they can plug into their power source on the job, and you won't learn whether or not they can do that by taking a survey.

Employee Engagement surveys are insulting to your employees, because you work among them and could simply walk up to them and ask "How's it going?" if the trust level were high enough for you to get a straight answer. If you haven't established enough trust through your actions that your employees would level with you face-to-face in the moment, then as my friend Joe the plumber says, "THERE's your problem!" Work on trust, ditch the surveys and save your money.

Most Expensive Business Scam Number Three: Process Improvement Fad of the Year

In the business world we are addicted to Process Improvement, but only the most fake and insulting kind. We give people new yardsticks to hit all the time. We love to implement new procedures, whether they make sense for the people using them or not.

We talk incessantly about usability when we're designing a website, but when the subject is internal process, we don't give a fig for the usability of the systems we devise.

We tell people do the same thing over and over all day long, as though they were machines instead of creative people, and then celebrate our success at replicating the process we invented, because our Six Sigma instructor told us that's what we should do.

I sat on a panel one time with a Lean expert who said that a certain set of faddish processes are the secret to healthy organizations. "What do the processes say about trust, about honesty in communication and about treating people with dignity?" I asked him. "All of those things are critical for implementation," he replied.

"That is odd," I said. "If Lean is a written standard, why would the three things I just mentioned, all critical for a successful implementation, be left out of the standard? Isn't a standard a roadmap for users to follow? If trust, honesty and dignity are essential for a system to succeed, how come they're not mentioned in the standard at all?"

It's because we have lost sight of the human element at work.

We pretend it doesn't exist. We pretend that people are parts of the machine, and that they'll do their jobs the way we tell them to because we're in charge and they're not.

We are seeing the limits of the people-as-machines dogma. We are realizing that we're being scammed. The scammers are laughing all the way to the bank. Our employees are fed up and sick to death of being poked and prodded and measured at every turn and talked down to like children.

When will our Board members and C-level leaders wake up and smell the coffee? It can only be good for them, for shareholders and for their customers when they do.

OTHER DEPARTMENTS ARE POACHING MY TEAM

Dear Liz,

I manage a 60-person department. My employees are financial analysts with two to five years of experience, who support more senior-level financial professionals in various units of our company.

I have worked hard to make our department a fun place to work, and we do a lot of peer-led training, so employees get to share what they know and take on more responsibility over time. I have always been happy to see my employees move on and up after they've spent a couple of years in my group.

Two of the Vice-Presidents in our company began their careers in the department I lead (before my arrival), in fact. But the "poaching" of my employees by other departments has become a real problem. I have a track record of hiring smart people, and now I see managers from other departments taking my new employees to lunch and generally beginning to sell them on other jobs as soon as they walk in the door.

To make matters worse, a couple of the folks I hired who were quickly pulled into other jobs flamed out in those jobs; ironically, they were told "you don't know enough about our analysis tools," although I'd had each of them in my group for less than six months.

I feel that some of the managers of other units in our company are treating my department as a training department, but making no investment in that training, and then complaining when the folks they steal from me haven't learned enough to be useful in more senior-level roles.

I am glad I'm providing a service to the company by hiring and training the "feeder crop" for other departments, but enough is enough. How can I get my fellow managers to back off and leave my employees alone, at least for a year or 18 months?

Thanks,
Janek

Dear Janek,

This is a great question, and it goes right to the heart of the leadership culture in your company. If your workplace follows a dog-eat-dog, every-manager-for-himself leadership philosophy, you may have an uphill battle getting your fellow managers to give you some breathing room with your new hires.

If you can show the company leaders and your HR chief how your "feeder crop" mechanism is important for the company, and remind them that pulling the seedlings out of the ground the minute they're planted is never a wise agricultural move, then you should be able to carve out some room to develop your people before they disappear.

I would start by compiling statistics to show how the rate of internal transfers out of your group has grown (if it has) over time. What you are doing under the present scheme is bearing the recruiting and training costs that your fellow managers would otherwise have to cover.

Some companies have a one-year requirement for internal transfers; that is, a newbie must stay in his or her original job for one year before another department can get their mitts on him or her. This is one way to limit your internal-transfer turnover and improve the odds that your new hires succeed in their future jobs.

However, I'd go further and get your HR leader and fellow managers involved in creating a feeder-crop system that supports everyone's goals. Maybe your expectation is 18 months for your new hires. If that's true, you can work with the other managers to make internal career opportunities available to your employees in an organized way that respects everyone's priorities.

You can start talking about those career opportunities even before your new employees take the job on your team. You can make the advancement potential part of your recruiting pitch.

The movement of employees throughout the organization is not the same as hiring someone from outside. Every employee deserves a contract and support for their development, but that's especially true when you hire people you hope to see advance within the company. Sit down with your fellow managers and work out a plan.

This is an important talent management topic that your leadership team can tackle as a group, if you can make the compelling case that the current ad hoc poaching scheme isn't benefitting anyone.

Cheers,
Liz

KPIS AND CORPORATE STUPIDITY

I worked for a long time in fast-growing companies, where people are moving too fast to stop and take measurements every five minutes. It wasn't until I started consulting that I saw just how much measurement of everyday tasks goes on in most large employers.

I was shocked. I met competent and smart people who spend as much time measuring their work as actually doing the work. I met very few people who felt good about the amount and type of measurement associated with their jobs.

"I have my real job, and then my extra job meeting the completely arbitrary numbers in my KPI Profile," said Marilyn, a veteran software engineer. "Tell me about the KPIs," I said.

"Key Performance Indicators," said Marilyn. "I have to keep track of about fifteen things that I do, and I have numbers to hit every week. The correlation between hitting my KPI targets and actually getting my work done is a very weak correlation. I could do a fantastic job during the week and move our company forward a lot and at the same time miss all my KPI targets."

"So, the yardsticks themselves are broken -- the measures," I suggested. "Not only that," said Marilyn, along with hundreds of other working people I've met over the years in similar circumstances. "It's not only that the yardsticks are poorly designed.

"There's no way any measurements could keep up with the changes in our business. We are on the front lines.

"The measurement-people are way at the back -- they are completely disconnected. We measure too much and there's too much emphasis on numbers. Why should I work hard to hit a number someone gave me? I work because my work is fun and challenging.

"It's insulting to have to stop my real work every few hours to focus on the numbers that someone assigned to me without even talking with me."

In the 'modern' business world based on a two-hundred-year-old industrial model, we are obsessed with measurement. We teach rising executives to make decisions based on numbers alone and we exalt some of the numbers by including them in Executive Dashboards. Reading a dashboard and making decisions based on numbers alone is the opposite of leadership.

I suppose you could captain a ship without actually being on the ship or seeing the water. You could simply read the numbers from the ship's instruments and make captain-type decisions that way, from a distance. Most of us would rather that our ship's captain stood right at the wheel and looked at the water and the sky.

Business is more about waves than particles, but many leaders can't get their heads out of spreadsheets long enough to notice the waves of energy swelling and crashing around them.

They are mystified by the topic "corporate culture" because it doesn't show up in their spreadsheet or on their dashboard, but it influences their success or failure more than any other factor.

When people feel like they're part of any win your firm might experience, they give everything they've got. Everyone knows that characteristic of humans, but in the business world we pretend that we don't know how humans operate. We pretend that they're motivated to hit the random KPI numbers we give them just because -- maybe because they're dying to get gold star on their forehead next week and the week after that and every week in the future.

We know better. If we trusted ourselves as leaders more than we do, we could get rid of half the goofy measurements we employ. We could stop obsessing about KPIs and talk about the mission, instead -- the organization's mission and our own personal missions bound up with it.

It's stupid to create lumbering bureaucratic systems just to measure your teammates' activities when the real goal is to take care of your customers and deliver great products and services. You'll never measure your way to greatness.

You'll never excite your team to higher heights by measuring them to death.

You'll never cultivate Team Energy by measuring more of your team's activities, but you can kill your culture by measuring too much and evaluating people based on their numbers more than other factors.

Team Energy is the momentum that powers a team to accomplish something amazing in business, athletics or anywhere people band together to achieve something great.

A healthy workplace is a place where the leaders understand the Passion-Performance Connection and don't shove KPIs down their teammates' throats just because they can.

They wouldn't dream of measuring anything non-essential or of slowing people down with excess measurements when there's so much real work to do.

That's why high-growth companies don't waste their time dreaming up KPIs. Who has time to stop and measure things when you're racing down your path?

Do you trust yourself enough to lead people without measuring every breath they take and every keystroke?

I hope you do -- because the time for a healthy workplace already here. It's a new day. Don't miss out on the benefits a trust-fueled culture gives you!

THE REAL REASON YOU'RE NOT ALLOWED TO WORK FROM HOME

When I became an HR person in 1984, every HR conference I attended included at least one session on Managing a Remote Workforce.

Back in 1984, everyone who studied the workplace predicted that most white-collar employees would be working from home or somewhere else — the beach or a coffee shop, for instance — by now.

All these years later, the prediction that most white-collar employees would be working from home and/or making their own schedule has not come true.

Before COVID-19, fewer than 25% of US-based white-collar workers were regularly working from home.

With so much technology available to make remote work faster, less expensive and more effective, why is this number so low?

Some large organizations (including Yahoo! when CEO Marissa Mayer took the helm) have pulled their formerly-flexible-workforces back into the office.

Why would a company tell employees "You may no longer work from home — come back and work in the office"?

Office space is expensive.

Back in the 1980s and 1990s, employers started realizing how expensive their office space was.

They started a practice called 'hoteling' where employees take an available workstation for the day when they are in the office, rather than having a fixed office or workstation of their own. Employers could cut down on office space that way.

Wouldn't it be cheaper for most or all employers to let their white-collar, Knowledge Worker employees work from home?

It would be cheaper. Most of us grew up learning that business is the art of investing wisely, but sometimes emotions overpower financial decision-making in the business world.

The real reason you're not allowed to work from home is that managers at all levels are fearful of change and especially fearful of change that requires them to step out of their comfort zone.

A leader whose employees work from home or from Starbucks has to trust their teammates. If the leader is fearful, the first way that fear will show itself is in the policies the leader hands down.

Leaders make their fear and trust levels clear in their words and even more so in their actions.

Leaders who cannot trust themselves enough to hire people they can trust will always revert to power and control mechanisms, including forcing people to drive a car or take a train to work every day so that their supervisors can keep an eye on them.

Those control mechanisms keep the leader's fear at bay.

Managers often say "I need my employees here in the office! That's where collaboration and teamwork spring up!"

In their hearts they know that collaboration and teamwork are things that spring up organically when people feel free to be themselves, and only then.

You will never get organic teamwork or collaboration out of people who are forced to be in a place they don't want to be.

The reason you're not allowed to work from home is that fear grips the corporate and institutional landscape, and many leaders are afraid to trust their employees whenever they're out of sight.

They may assume that an employee who's working from home is watching TV soap operas and eating bon-bons instead of getting their work done.

That lack of trust in themselves is a failure of leadership, and it hurts communities and individuals as well as the organization's own customers and shareholders.

Clearing roads and highways of morning and afternoon commuters would be good for the planet, as well as the physical and emotional health of commuters.

Allowing employees to work from home would give them better life/work balance, more chances to stretch during the day and a less hectic environment in which to have big ideas.

Your customers need and expect you to staff your organization with people who are charged-up and set free to accomplish great things.

Your customers would not approve of a leadership style that only trusts your own hand-picked employees when they are right in front of you!

It's time to ease up on your fear and let your employees work from home. You can begin with a pilot project and expand your work-from-home options from there.

It is time to step out of managerial fear and trust the people you hired to run your company.

If you can't trust the people you carefully vetted and selected from a group of qualified candidates, who can you trust?

If you don't trust yourself to lead, why should any customer, employee or shareholder trust you?

I LOVE HR PEOPLE, BUT I HATE THEIR JOB TITLES

I am an HR person. I know how hard it is to please hundreds or thousands of employees. Let's face it, people can get whiny. You can't walk ten feet down the hall as an HR person without having someone say to you "At my old job they treated us better. They gave us our birthday off with pay."

You have to bite your lip in half to prevent your tongue and teeth from saying "Why don't you go back there, then?"

You bite your lip all day long! Still, HR is an awesome field. I love it. I love HR people, too, but I hate the language they use.

HR people have some of the worst titles ever invented.

An all-purpose HR person has a critical job. His or her job is to listen to and take care of the employees so they can focus on their own jobs. Human problems crop up in any organization, and someone has to sort them out so the team can keep moving.

There are a million human ways to describe that job. Here are just a few of them:

- HR Consultant

- HR Coach

- HR Advocate

- HR Advisor

What does your embedded HR person do, after all? They listen. Sometimes the local HR Consultant has an answer right away, and sometimes they have to talk to other people to get the information an employee needs.

Sometimes the HR Coach spots issues that need resolution and digs into them, without anyone asking them for help.

We would have an easier time assigning HR titles if we weren't so fixated on the activities we think define the HR function: Training, Recruiting, Compensation and so on. Those activities are means to an end. They are ways to get your teammates he information and support they need to do their jobs. Why would you saddle your most employee-facing person, the HR Advisor, with the awful title HR Generalist or HR Business Partner?

If you're going to do that, why not go whole hog and call your CEO "Business Generalist?" The CEO has a high-altitude mission: to set a vision for the organization and lead the people there. Of necessity, a CEO is a generalist. Why is that title only used in HR?

Your HR Consultant has a noble mission, too. They have to (& get to) to remove all impediments that might keep your team from racing down the field. They consult with managers, employees and other HR folks. Why not call them a Consultant, an Advisor or a Coach given that that's what they do?

Another awful HR title is Strategic Business Partner. The first rule of strategy if that if you are doing strategic things, you don't have the word "Strategic" in your title.

Your CFO has a strategic job. Do they have "Strategic" in his or her title? Nope!

HR Strategic Business Partners are like HR Generalists, although I hope that if you have either of those titles, you insist on a new title immediately. The first rule of partnership is that you don't become a partner by putting the word "Partner" on your business card.

If people want to partner with you, they know how to find you. Here's what partnership is: partnership is Morry and Solly, who met on the boat from Eastern Europe to Manhattan in 1905 and when they landed, started a deli together. Their great-grandchildren are still running the deli today. They are true partners. They found one another and started something cool.

HR people have an important job to do, and that job is not running around looking for people willing to partner with them. How come your IT and Finance people don't have "partner" in their titles? They don't need to. They perform a vital service to the organization, and everyone knows what it is.

They don't need to pander by putting words like "Strategic" and "Partner" in their titles. And let's not forget the word "Business!"

Why would HR people want the word "Business" in their titles? More pandering! That's to let people know that they are businesspeople, in case anyone might be confused that HR people are zookeepers or hairstylists who wandered into the wrong building.

In a healthy workplace the role of HR is obvious and fundamental. HR leaders are Ministers of Culture. Their job is to keep the energy moving in the organization, to spread the critically important cultural pixie dust that makes an organization hum.

If you don't see pixie dust, you might have trouble seeing the vital work that HR people do. That is your energetic impairment. If you can't see anything that isn't on a spreadsheet or a bar chart, I feel sorry for you. You will not become a great leader until you learn to read between the lines, the way your valiant HR champions do every day.

THE EMPLOYEE ENGAGEMENT HOAX

When I became an HR person, we talked about *employee morale*. As an HR person I was very concerned with the question "How is the team doing?"

If people were upset about something -- an overly restrictive policy, a change in work hours or a cut in benefits, for instance - I had to know about it, and to respond.

If people aren't happy at work, there will be repercussions. Turnover is the most obvious one, but there are worse effects of poor morale than turnover, which at least happens in the visible universe. You can tell when someone quits.

When people decide to stop trying, when they're frustrated and angry at work, you can feel the negative energy in the organization. Customers can feel it. It shows itself in the quarterly results and the annual report. It wouldn't be an overstatement to say that the first priority for any HR person (and every leader) is to make sure that the people on the team feel valued, listened-to and equipped to do their jobs without artificial constraints or impediments.

Somewhere around the late 1980s or early 1990s we stopped talking about employee morale and started talking about Employee Engagement instead. It wasn't until the year 2000 that I fully got the absurdity of the Employee Engagement concept. It happened this way:

I was having lunch with a former colleague of mine who was working for a telephone carrier in 2000, one of the spin-offs from the Ma Bell divestiture. The company was in turmoil at the time of our lunch -- people were being laid off right and left, and the CEO was under investigation. (He later went to jail.) I asked my former workmate "How's morale in the company?"

She said "We don't talk about morale anymore. We talk about *engagement with the mission.*"

My hand and fork stopped midway between plate and mouth as I lifted my eyes to catch hers. Was she putting me on? Nope -- she was deadly serious. "Wait a second," I said. "You're laying people off. They're dropping like flies. Every two weeks there's another reduction in force. If you believe that people operate in their own self-interest, you'd have to wonder how anybody could give a hoot about the company's mission when they might be out of work two weeks from now - wouldn't you?"

"We expect them to engage with the mission," my ex-colleague icily replied. "That's the best way for them to stay employed."

Somehow the time-honored concept of employee morale -- the answer to the question "How's the team doing?" got twisted into the notion of Employee Engagement, where the penalty for being insufficiently *engaged with the mission* is to be responsible for one's own layoff.

At that moment in the year 2000 I realized that toxic-lemonade-drunk HR people (or any working person) can buy into the fiction that it's every employee's duty to put the interests of the company's mission ahead of his or her own interests. (What mission that might be was never made clear to the team or to anyone -- I know that because, like everyone in my state, I was a customer of the telephone company.)

What an utter crock, I thought to myself, but didn't say out loud. I had already learned the lesson that it's pointless to argue with people who are brainwashed.

Employee engagement is a made-up concept that exists solely to make leaders and HR people feel as though they've really got an ear to the ground, even in cases where no such careful listening exists.

The most common invocation of the term Employee Engagement is in the annual Employee Engagement survey, an insulting ritual. Once a year, we give the team a form to fill out, even though we spent the better part of every day working alongside and among them. At any moment, any supervisor could ask "So Stan, how's it going? How is the job working out for you? Anything I need to know? Anything I can do?"

We don't do that, but we send out a survey and let the prisoners know that once a year they can scribble on a form and slip it through a narrow slot in the cell. That's the opposite of the Minister of Culture role every HR person and leader should exemplify. Our employees have individual stories, ideas and insights to share, but we tell them "Wait until it's time to complete the survey" rather than tune in to the rich and contextual wisdom they're offering us every single day, if we had the time to listen.

Would we tell our customers when we're standing beside them, "Please hold your feedback for the annual Customer Satisfaction survey!"? We would not, unless we want to lose our customers. We're all ears when we're trying to make a sale or keep a customer happy. Employees don't get the same consideration.

Employee Engagement falls into the vast category of Junk Science so beloved in the business world. There is no single construct called Employee Engagement, certainly not one that applies across functions and levels, but we pretend that there is, and then, like good weenie businesspeople the world over, we measure the heck out of it. Employee Engagement Surveys are constructed and peddled by vendors who prey on the fear of HR leaders who don't want to be held responsible for bad marks on any yardstick.

The chief benefit of the annual Employee Engagement Survey is that it lets a tone-deaf HR leader say to her leadership team, "Look how high our engagement scores are this year! Surely I'm doing my job!"

If we want to listen to our employees for real, we won't send out once-a-year surveys. We'll fling open doors all over the joint and make it easy for employees to tell us when things are going well and when they're not. Here are 12 of the hundreds of ways we can listen to our teammates if we care about more than getting a passing grade on a cynical, once-a-year 'listening' exercise:

1. We can hold Town Hall meetings, live or virtual, where employees can ask questions in real time or submit them in advance and get answers from their local leaders and the organization's executives.

2. We can schedule executive visits to department staff meetings where leaders can have more personal, small-group conversations with specific teams about their most pressing issues.

3. We can establish a confidential 1-800 hotline that employees can use to report urgent problems like theft, violence, sexual harassment or discrimination, or unsafe conditions.

4. We can hire roving HR people who ask "What's new? How's your workload? How are you doing?" as routinely and organically as supervisors ask "When will that report be completed?"

5. We can create a widely-publicized, universally-accessible email account and web contact form that employees can use to share concerns, ask questions and get help with anything that's blocking their forward motion, from an unclear or unevenly-applied policy to a rogue manager's behavior.

6. We can organize quarterly one-on-one lunches (offsite) between each manager and one employee, where the two of them can dig into any topic that requires discussion and can't be handled in the course of a normal workday.

7. We can install an executive-level Chief Listening Officer whose job (exclusively or not, based on the size of the firm) is to make sure that good ideas get to the top of the

organization and that problems get addressed quickly and resolved.

8. We can designate a company-wide agenda item to appear at the top of every staff meeting, new employee orientation, leadership development and training meeting and every other time and place where employees gather. The agenda item is a five-to-ten-minute discussion on the topic "How are we doing?" When managers are told it's okay to talk about the energy in a workplace and when their attention to the needs of the team is reinforced at every level, the practice will take hold.

9. We can establish a voicemail account just for suggestions and high-priority issues or complaints, like a Suggestion Box by phone. With so many priorities to address in the course of a business day, the easier it is to report a problem or promote a suggestion at the instant one thinks of it, the better.

10. We can provide training throughout the organization in listening, probing for information and interpersonal communication, so badly needed and so often lacking in large organizations.

11. We can see that our CEO frequently, vocally and specifically reinforces the message "Our culture is everything, and our team creates our success." If the emphasis on trust is real, the CEO will talk about it. If it's lip service, everyone will know it.

12. We can offer fast, human acknowledgement of problems when they occur, instead of hasty cover-ups and fog. Actions, as the wise person said, speak louder than words.

Employee Engagement and the survey mentality glued to its hip are hoaxes of the first degree. Any employee with a smidgen of emotional awareness can spot the falsity of the check-a-box feedback exercise from a mile away. Employers who want to hear what their employees think have plenty of ways to get that priceless information. All they have to do is really, truly ask and be ready to listen. Managing through trust is simpler, faster and much less expensive than managing through fear, but tossing a pointless Employee Engagement survey out to the masses once a year is an easy way to pretend that you care, when it's obvious that you don't.

FOUR WAYS YOU'RE
RELINQUISHING YOUR POWER --
WITHOUT REALIZING IT

We use the word "power" a lot at work. In any organization, we know that certain people have more power than other people do.

We know which people are more powerful than we are — high-level executives, for instance. We tend to watch what we say and how we act around powerful people.

Most of us have been taught a twisted and unhealthy definition of power.

We've been taught that someone is powerful because they have a fancy job title and earn a lot of money. We tend to focus on one kind of power, but there are two different kinds — and they couldn't be more different.

One kind of power is the kind other people confer on you when they promote you to a high-level position or give you some other honor.

The power that other people bestow on you is not real power — it is borrowed from the person or institution that bestowed it.

That's why one of the weakest ways to brand yourself is to talk about the lofty educational institutions you graduated from, and the blue-chip employers you worked for.

When you brand yourself by telling the world that these well-regarded companies and institutions found you to be acceptable, you do yourself a disservice.

You are not smart or worthy because you graduated from an Ivy League college or worked for a company whose name everyone knows. You are powerful because of who you are. Your degrees, past job titles, budgets, staff sizes, awards and accolades are just icing on the cake!

One kind of power is conferred on you by other people. They can give you power and they can just as easily take it away.

The much more important kind of power is the kind you build in yourself. When I talk about growing your flame, I am talking about becoming more powerful as a person — no matter what your job title is and no matter where you've worked before or where you went to school.

You carry the most important kind of power around with you. Your power grows when you say or do the right thing, especially when you're the only person saying or doing the right thing.

Your power shrinks when you go along with a bad or unethical idea just because everybody else seems to like it.

Your power grows when you take a step into new territory. The harder it is to step out of your comfort zone and try something that seems a little scary, the more powerful you will become just by doing it!

Your power diminishes when you act out of fear. Here are four ways you may be giving away your power without realizing it:

Rising to Your Own Defense

When your professional opinion is contradicted or a co-worker challenges you, it is tempting to jump to your own defense — but very often that is the wrong thing to do.

If someone insults you or puts you down at work, your best bet may be to stay silent. The person who attacked you will be viewed as unprofessional and immature for engaging in schoolyard-type bullying. You don't need to stoop to their level!

Your ability to stay calm, rise above the fray and listen to criticism (fair or unfair) without reacting is a testament to your character.

Engaging in Gossip

When you're upset with your boss, a co-worker or anyone else at work, you can ask a workplace friend to listen to your story and counsel you on the best response. However, to solve the problem you will eventually need to talk to your boss or co-worker directly, rather than complaining about them behind their back.

When you engage in workplace gossip, you give your power away. You tell yourself, your conversation partner and the whole universe that you are too fearful to address your concerns head-on, so you're gossiping about someone instead. Don't squander your precious power that way!

Changing Your Behavior to Please Your Boss — Or Anyone Else You're Afraid Of

Almost all of us have had the experience of hearing ourselves speak at work and wondering "Who the heck is speaking? When did I start saying things like that? I can't believe these words are coming out of my mouth!"

We might even lie in bed at night and think about the workday — and realize that we didn't tell the truth at work, because we were trying so hard to please the people around us.

If you have to contort yourself into pretzel shapes at work to please your boss or anyone else, it is not the right job for you. You have two choices. Little by little, you can test your growing muscles and speak more of your truth at work — or you can start job-hunting.

Many people find that job-hunting on the side give them enough moral support that they start to feel more comfortable being honest at work.

Launching a part-time stealth job search is a fantastic way to grow your flame!

Letting People Get Under Your Skin

The last way to give up your power for no benefit is to let people around you at work make you mad or get you to feel bad about yourself.

Some people love to get their co-workers riled up. They seek to make their teammates or subordinates upset because it makes them feel better. That is a fear-based behavior that is common at work.

Don't let people get under your skin. If someone makes you mad, bite your lip until it bleeds if necessary, and say to yourself in your mind "That's okay — that person is feeling fearful right now. Their rude comment has nothing to do with me — it's just an indication of their state of mind at this moment."

My young friend Sasha ran into this situation at work not long ago.

She designed a magnificent promotional piece for an event her company was hosting.

At her department's weekly staff meeting, Sasha passed around copies of the promotional piece while her co-workers oohed and aahed.

One of them said "Sasha, you are incredibly talented!"

Another colleague said "This is going to get so many registrations in the door! Way to go, Sasha!"

One of Sasha's co-workers, Allan, sat sullen and silent at the end of the table.

When the positive reaction to Sasha's promotional piece had died down, Allan finally spoke.

"This isn't bad work, Sasha," he said, "but I could help you get a lot better at designing pieces like this. Let me know if you want me to teach you sometime."

Sasha wanted to say something brilliant and cutting, but a voice spoke up in her mind.

"Allan is horrified to see that you are as capable as you are, Sasha," said the voice.

"Let it go. Don't let him bug you."

Sasha smiled and took a sip of her coffee. The meeting went on.

Later on, her manager said "Sasha, I know it must have bugged you when Allan made that remark about how he could teach you to design better marketing pieces. I applaud you for letting that remark roll off your back. At the right time, I will talk with Allan about his communication skills."

"It's okay," Sasha told her manager.

"Sometimes we say things without thinking. I don't hold it against Allan."

Sasha told me later "Little by little, I am growing my flame. I am paying close attention to the things people say out of trust, and the things they say and do out of fear. I know there's a lot of fear in the workplace, and I am not immune to it either. If I keep paying attention and noticing fear and trust around me, then other people's fearful remarks and attitudes won't bother me so much."

The same is true for you.

Let fearful people work through their fear on their own — don't give them something to push against.

Keep your power for yourself. You will need it to fuel your brilliant adventure

TIME OFF: THE EUROPEANS DO IT RIGHT

Twenty years ago, I was living on the road - way more than was healthy. We expect to see 25-year-old management consultants living out of suitcases, but when you're in your 30s and have small children at home, a heavy business travel schedule is a major encumbrance.

Two weeks every year, if I were lucky, I'd get to pack up the kids and the gear and take a family vacation. But there was a problem: The work didn't stop.

Even when I was hiking in the mountains or sitting on the beach, counting heads bobbing in the waves, my phone would ring. My husband would glower. My heart would sink, because I feared it meant something was up at the office.

I'd pick up the phone and be dragged into an hour-long call. I'd be flashing the five-finger hand sign to my husband (as in, "five more minutes") but the call would drag on and on. I'd think, "Something is wrong with the system."

The System Never Sleeps

Ironically, during the same years that I was trying to take real vacations and mostly failing, I scoffed and turned up my nose at the European schedule whereby whole populations vacation at the same time of year. My company's French facilities would shut down in August.

No contact, no work, no one's home, they're all off on holiday. Like a typical American, I'd shake my head. "How can you compete in the marketplace when the whole company disappears for a month?" my American workmates and I would say. And then we'd get in the car or on a plane and take a fake American vacation where the phone never stops ringing.

The truth is that the Europeans got it right. In the knowledge economy, the only way to free yourself from your work is to conspire with your colleagues to put everything on hold. Think of those old Looney Tunes cartoons where the cat chases the mouse, and then they both stop and take a break and then they start the chase all over again. We're adults. We can agree: no work in August. We could pick any month. But when we go away and the work keeps coming, no one benefits.

Our families suffer because we're only half with them when we're on vacation, waiting for that phone to ring. We bring our laptops to the beach (and get sand in them). Our commitments aren't daily or weekly, they're ongoing: This report is due, it's budget time, the Monday meeting must have minutes, and you're the only one who can write them. Our work doesn't give us room to enjoy our time off, even though the payroll records show that we've earned it.

Vacation Solidarity!

My husband used to ask me, "Don't they understand you're on vacation?" It was hard for me to get him to understand.

"They're my friends, and I don't want to let them down," I'd say. "I can ignore the phone, but my own performance results and my friends' results would suffer. No one is forcing me to pick up the phone or answer the e-mail, but it's an ethical obligation, because I can't throw my colleagues under the bus."

"Then something is goofed up in the system," he'd say, and he was right.

Americans take slightly more than half of the vacation time they earn every year, and they aren't earning all that much. It's hard to go on vacation. There's an assembly line moving, and when you desert your spot, the units don't stop coming at you. These days, they're knowledge units and budget units and product-launch units instead of car parts, but they don't stop and they don't slow down just because you're on holiday.

Since we're not likely to adopt the European schedule any time soon, we may have to agree with our workmates on our vacation philosophies instead.

If we say to one another, "I'm going to Yosemite, and I'm going to disappear for a week, no contact," then they can prepare for that. We may still feel pangs of guilt if we see their phone numbers popping up on our cell-phone screens and don't answer their calls, but hey, we warned them.

A half-vacation is no rest at all, and we deserve those few weeks of mental rest every year. If you practice the full-separation vacation a few times in the U.S., you may even work yourself up to a 100%-disconnected trip to France. Just don't go in August—it's packed with tourists then.

PERFORMANCE REVIEWS ARE POINTLESS AND INSULTING -- SO WHY DO THEY STILL EXIST?

Dear Liz,

I'm the HR Director for a growing manufacturing firm. I started the job in July. I report to the CEO.

I'm putting my plan together for next year. One thing I told my boss "Jake" when he interviewed me is that I plan to talk him out of the company's annual performance-review process.

I agree with you that making every employee fill out an evaluation form and sit down to talk about it every year is a huge waste of time and energy, and most employees hate performance reviews.

If the relationship is healthy between the manager and the employee, they're having regular conversations anyway — including quarterly and annual planning sessions. If that isn't happening, I can help managers fix that -- but having more conversations doesn't require an evaluation process

I eliminated performance reviews at my last company and everyone was happy about it.

Of course, employees need to be able to get feedback when they need it. If they can get that feedback without being graded like elementary school students, it's a win-win for everybody.

Jake says he might be open to the idea of abolishing performance reviews, but he needs a very good reason to do so. In my last company I polled our managers (37 of them) and 35 were in favor of getting rid of performance reviews.

The other two managers were neutral. We knew the employees were negative about the performance review process because the subject came up regularly in our Town Hall Meetings and survey responses.

Jake wants me to write up a proposal for him. Thanks in advance for any insights you can share!

Yours,
Haze

Dear Haze,

Performance reviews are artifacts left over from the Industrial Revolution.

They come from an earlier time, when work was designed on the mechanical model I call Godzilla.

If employees stand in front of a conveyor belt all day polishing widgets, you can easily count the widgets as they come down the line and see which employees are hitting their goals and which folks are missing them.

Knowledge Work is more complex and nuanced than that. Knowledge Worker jobs don't boil down to a number of widgets polished per hour or per quarter.

Somebody on your team might have a breakthrough idea today precisely because they ignored the passing parade of widgets and stared off into space for 45 minutes.

That's the energy you want to inspire and capture in your company — not widget-polishing energy!

Performance reviews are not effective at improving performance. They have never shown their value as leadership tools -- but they make excellent power-and-control mechanisms, and that is one reason some companies have trouble giving up on them.

It doesn't help an employee move forward for a manager to tell them what they did well and did badly last year. If a manager needs to give someone feedback, they should do that in the moment — not months later.

When we are lifted up in the service of a larger goal than to hit our weekly and quarterly numbers, we don't need to waste time rating and grading employees. We only need to reinforce them and give them room to run!

We need every millisecond of our time and energy to be spent inspiring and encouraging our teammates — not to mention moving obstacles out of their way.

Here are five reasons performance reviews are a waste of time:

1. They take up expensive staff hours for no observable gain. It takes hours and hours of time for employees and managers to complete performance review forms, get them approved, set up performance review meetings and handle the paperwork. The next year, they do it all over again.

   Who benefits from that massive time and energy investment? Do your customers benefit? They don't — because if there were customer-benefiting information to be shared it would have happened whenever it came to light, not now.

2. Their purpose is unclear — and always has been. Various people will tell you that performance reviews are essential for letting employees know how they're doing (why?), to justify pay increases (you don't need performance reviews for that), or to create a paper trail if someone should need to be terminated (doesn't work, because managers almost always give struggling employees average-to-good

performance reviews. Later they say, "I was trying to motivate the employee!").

Anything you might want to accomplish through performance reviews can be accomplished without them.

3. They are unfair. Companies come up with rigid systems (five-point review scales and ten-point scales!) but they never solve the biggest rating challenge — the fact that managers vary dramatically in their assessments of Excellent, Good, Average, Fair and Needs Improvement. Performance reviews are also unfair because they tend to weight more recent events and results more heavily than those from earlier in the year. They are unfair because managers have biases.

4. Performance reviews are insulting. If I hire someone to work for me doing graphic design, marketing strategy or software development I can talk to them about the project and our relationship. I can let them know if I'm unhappy with something they do or don't do, but it's not my place to tell them how to do their job or how to live their life.

    Performance reviews cement the bad, old idea that when someone is your supervisor, they sit on a higher plane than you do. That's ridiculous. A supervisor in today's Knowledge Economy is an orchestral conductor. The conductor keeps the orchestra together but doesn't presume to tell the musicians how to play their instruments.

5. Every business process requires a clear objective and desired outcome, to pay its way in your busy operation. Performance reviews lack both a clear objective and a desired outcome. No one in your company can say "Here's the outcome we want when we conduct performance reviews next year."

There is no desired outcome except to remind the employees who's a boss and who isn't — and to keep up a time-honored tradition simply because you've always done it.

Talk to your fellow managers and employees and see what they think about performance reviews.

If you can't find anybody ready to defend performance reviews, tell Jake "I didn't hear from anyone who wanted to keep performance reviews going.

"This is our opportunity to streamline our company, save money, act on our team members' feedback and shift our culture out of old-fashioned command and control management into new-millennium leadership!"

Most managers, like most employees, fear change.

CEOs fear change, too. Tell Jake you'll use the coming year as a test year to see if your organization falls apart when you ditch performance reviews. I predict that like every other company that has done away with them, you'll be much happier when they're gone!

Yours,
Liz

PART THREE

TRUST & CORPORATE CULTURE

WORK IS BROKEN – BUT IT'S FIXABLE

I don't know where the lady got my cellphone number, but I heard the phone ringing in my purse as I stepped into a cab, and I grabbed it and answered it without looking at the number.

"Is this Liz?" asked the lady.

"Yes," I said. "I'm sorry that I don't recognize your number."

"Oh, my CEO gave me your number," she said. "We have some organizational things going on, and my boss, the company CEO, wants to have you work with our team."

"OK," I said. "Can you tell me a little about what's going on?"

"Oh," she sighed, "discord and unhappiness, some complainers, people upset with my boss, you know."

"I'm sorry to hear about it," I said. "It sounds frustrating."

"My boss told me to call you and tell you, 'Make it stop,' in fact," said the poor woman.

"It is draining for everyone when there's a disturbance in the Force like that," I said.

"You said it!" said my caller. "You will make my boss very happy if you come out here and fix it. He even told me to tell you that he's prepared to get rid of every one of them, but I'm not sure if he was joking when he said that or serious."

"I understand," I said. "I'd love to meet your CEO when he has time."

"That won't be necessary," said the well-meaning lady. "I just wanted to make sure that you're available on the dates we have in mind for your visit, and then I'll introduce you to our HR director. The assignment is to work with the executives and coach them on how to be a team. The CEO won't be there."

"I apologize, I'm just between meetings," I said. "Why don't you send me an email message with your thoughts. I should tell you, just to save your time, that I won't be able to work with your team unless the CEO is in the conversation too. I don't mean that he has to be in every meeting with his staff. There will be times when I'd like to talk with the staff without the CEO there. I will need to meet and work with the CEO, however. It's his team, after all."

"Oh, my!" said the administrative assistant. "That is not going to happen. He wants help for the leadership team, not for himself. He told me to take care of the problem by the end of the quarter."

And there you have it.

When people ask me, "What is a Human Workplace™ anyway?" I tell them that it isn't a place where they have free drinks and popcorn and people get to go home early, although those things are fine by me. It's a place where people are human.

In the real world we know that a leader — in Cub Scouts, on a high school volleyball team or anywhere — is part of a team and a more influential member than any other person. In business we pretend that that isn't the case. "Fix my team but leave me out of it" is the second most common conversation stopper we hear. (The most common conversation stopper is "we need you to find us some rock stars and ninjas, but we're not interested in looking at our recruiting process.")

When an organization (a company, a government agency, a not-for-profit or any entity) decides to follow the Human Workplace™ path, they start by telling the truth about the human and inhuman issues swirling around them. They talk about what's going well and what's crashing and burning. They talk about energy and notice where the energy is moving fast and where it's blocked and dammed up.

They take responsibility for their piece of the puzzle. They don't believe that being a leader means being divorced from the action.

They acknowledge that the only thing that powers their ideas, their product features, their newsletters, their inventory turns, and their investor-pleasing numbers are the good ideas and good will of their employees, contractors, vendors and customers.

No one in the community is left out of that circle.

When we transactionalize the relationships around us such that we forget that the other people in the mix are people first and whatever else they are (customers, bankers, employees or job seekers, for instance) second, we destroy our chance of building a healthier organization. When we start with the premise that we are fine ourselves and therefore would only ever dream of surrounding ourselves with other fine, smart, funny, creative and whole people, we begin to build the right energy in our own shop and in the working world in general.

It is a very easy thing to do, but you have to shed old ideas to do it. You have to give up the idea that the boss is righter than anyone else. You have to let go of the notion that because you pay someone, you control him or her. It is a strange and twisted idea that when we pay a person for his or her services, we also get to (or would even want to) control that person's connection to the power source, to the fount of creativity.

We don't tell the miller how to mill the flour (if we dealt with millers, that is). Why would things be any different in the case of our database administrator? If we don't trust a person to do his or her job, why did we hire that person?

We can build a better workplace when we notice and emphasize trust over fear, and when we practice giving up control. Leaders who understand that people connected to their power source will always bring more, deliver more, think bigger, have sparkier ideas and create more exciting results will win. But leaders who dwell in the realm of policies and restrictions, protocols and red tape and controls in the vain hope that those things will keep them safe from their nameless fear that some horrible thing might happen? Those guys always fail.

My old boss, Jon Zakin, used to say, "You can't save your way to greatness." Nor can you administer your way to greatness, or employee-handbook your way to greatness, or process-control your way there. Greatness comes when people attach to a vision and make it their own. There's no carrot and no stick that can produce that spark and that voltage.

You build a healthy workplace by gently, continually breaking down the barriers that keep people from connecting to their work and thereby keep them from giving a shit about your yardsticks and your gold stars. In our company we have a name for the edifice of rules, controls, hierarchy and fear that blocks the energy in so many organizations right now.

We call the edifice Godzilla, after the Blue Oyster Cult song. ("History shows again and again how nature points out the folly of men. Godzilla!")

We can break down Godzilla, bit by bit, with as much zeal as pursuing a new acquisition or a market segment. We only have to trust ourselves to trust the people we surround ourselves with, and to be human with them.

The CEO in the apocryphal story at the top of this piece isn't a bad guy, I'm sure. He just doesn't see his role in the soap opera of dysfunction that he brought into being. He wants things to change, but he wants the system to stay the same.

That's not rational thinking, but we have trained ourselves to think irrationally in business, and, worse, to teach other people to do the same. It's not too late for that to change. It only takes remembering that we are humans, and no algorithm, edict or strategic plan can alter that.

HOW TO KILL YOUR TEAM'S MOTIVATION WITHOUT REALLY TRYING

There is a multi-billion-dollar 'motivation' industry that feeds on the fact that most people don't know what strong leadership looks like, or how to emulate it.

Companies bring in consultants to 'improve the team's motivation.' What a waste of time!

Nobody comes to work to do a bad job. We all want to use our brains and hearts, but too often corporate or institutional rules, hierarchy, conflict, lack of planning or bureaucratic fear get in our way. Naturally our motivation plummets then!

You don't need motivation programs to get people excited. A motivation program is an artificial answer to a man-made problem.

We have been raised on fear-based management, on the carrot and the stick. It's the only kind of management most of us know. We're so used to it that we don't see how it hurts us every day to treat our employees like children instead of the talented and capable adults they are.

Thinking adults don't need rewards to spur them on or punishments to correct their bad habits. Those methods are insulting and ineffective. They are heavy-handed. When you simply hire people you trust and set them loose to amaze you, they will!

We have lost sight of a manager's true job, which is not to push people to hit arbitrary goals on a yardstick. Who would ever be motivated to do that?

We don't see the pivotal role that a manager plays in his or her team's success. We even discipline employees for being insufficiently motivated, as though anybody likes to get up and come to work to be bored and thwarted. Job ads say, "We want to hire a motivated self-starter!"

Here's the problem with the idea that you can simply hire 'motivated' people, then sit back and watch them work: motivation is a function of your environment.

It isn't something that your employees carry around with them, like a tape measure. Motivation programs are an expensive distraction and a waste of time. You can't prod and poke people into being motivated. You certainly won't motivate anybody by criticizing them.

The good news is that it's easy to bring out your team's natural motivation to solve problems when their work is interesting and worth doing, and when they are given the tools, time and latitude to do a great job.

All you have to do to tap the amazing power supply your teammates bring to work with them is to take away the barriers to forward motion that most organizations erect without meaning to.

Some organizations make it nearly impossible for a team member to move forward an inch. They don't trust their employees enough to let them do the jobs they were hired for.

Here are ten roadblocks to forward energy you can start to dismantle immediately. The more easily you allow the energy to flow in your shop, the more easily your team will reach its goals!

Ten Energy Blockers That Kill Motivation

MURKY OR NONEXISTENT PLAN

When there's no plan, nobody knows what the plan is or the plan changes every two weeks, you can kiss your team's motivation good-bye.

ROLE CONFUSION

In a healthy organization roles may be flexible, but your team won't get far if more than one person feels they are responsible for the same things or if there are chunks of your mission that no one is responsible for.

MIXED MESSAGES

You can't tell your team they are the industry's best and then cut their tuition benefits or their lunch hour the next day. Mixed messages send the loud message "Our manager's support is mostly lip service."

UNADDRESSED CONFLICT

You won't make conflicts go away by ignoring them. Honor everyone in the mix and don't designate winners and losers as you resolve conflicts. Keep your team's good energy in mind!

LACK OF VISIBILITY

When your teammates have no idea where the organization is trying to go or how their team can help get there, how can they care? Everybody needs visibility into the future. Your job as a manager is to get your team the information, they need to make good decisions.

ELEPHANT IN THE ROOM

An elephant in the room is an important topic that should get airtime but does not get it. No one wants to talk about the elephant in the room, so everyone pretends not to see it.

RED TAPE

Red tape is excess bureaucracy. It chokes the life out of a team. Most organizations have way too many policies – so many that most of them are ignored. Don't write any more policies -- get rid of some policies, instead!

TOO MANY APPROVALS

When your employees can't take a breath without getting signatures from God and the Dalai Lama, something is broken.

DISTURBANCE IN THE FORCE

A disturbance in the force is a negative change in the energy field -- such as your team's chilly reaction to a new bonus plan. Talk about it and get things straightened out! "I can't change the policy" is not something that a real manager says. "Let me start a conversation and see what happens, and keep you posted" is a step in the right direction.

BURNOUT

Burnout is a stone-cold trust killer. You have choices: you can ease up on the workload or watch your teammates wither on the vine and give up.

As a manager you can choose to ignore any or all of these energy blockers, and many managers do just that. They don't believe that they can fix their team's problems, so they pretend the problems don't exist. They try to manage through the thick sludge that gums up their processes, communication and daily life at work.

You won't great ideas from beaten-down, exhausted or frustrated people.

You won't get innovation or collaboration from them. The most you can hope for is grudging compliance. As a manager, is your mission to wring grudging compliance from your teammates, or to inspire them to new heights?

When we are fearful of rocking the boat, we pretend that we can manage our teammates just by telling them what their goals are and letting the mechanism of fear do the rest of our job for us.

What is the mechanism of fear? It's the unspoken but well-understood relationship between doing your job and having an income. We lead through fear when we assume that people must care about their work because if they don't care, they'll get fired.

You can't bully or threaten people into caring about their work, even if the threats are passive ones.

It is time for us to tell the truth about fear and trust and to bring ourselves to work every day. We can't keep pretending that forecasts and budgets make our companies go, when we know in our hearts that it's only the commitment and goodwill of our teammates that makes anything worthwhile happen.

It is a new day, and we can tell the truth about the currents of fear and trust swirling around us at work. We have to, if we value our customers, our shareholders, our teammates and our own health.

We can find our voices and speak up about what's working and what isn't working in our organizations. We can start today!

INTERNAL COMMUNICATION: FROM THE PODIUM TO THE PAYSTUB

As a corporate HR person for over twenty years and a consultant for lots more, I've had a great chance to observe organizations with an anthropological eye.

From the moment you walk through the revolving door into a business office until the time you leave, you pick up a hundred little clues as to how the organization operates and what it values. For internal communicators, it's just as important to pay attention to these subtle messages as it is to design an award-winning communications strategy. Here's why.

When you ask yourself "What are we saying throughout this organization, and what do we want to say?" you will quickly come up with a list of themes, initiatives, and values that you currently promote.

You'll look at employee communication materials, internal newsletters, your company's website, your events and lots of other vehicles that you hope are doing the "heavy lifting" of internal communication for you.

You'll be able to spot the gaps between what you DO say and what you WANT to say to your team. So far, so good.

But evaluating the published materials and beautifully designed website content misses the point.

Employees are very sophisticated when it comes to evaluating internal messaging. They can quickly spot the difference between the Party Line and the Way Things Really Work.

That's why internal communicators who focus on the formal vehicles risk missing the channels that speak most loudly to employees.

For instance, you can talk about risk-taking until you're blue in the face, featuring risk-taking employees in your internal newsletter and giving awards to people who went out on a limb.

But the first time your employees hear about the CEO or another senior leader bashing someone (or worse, firing them) for taking a risk that didn't pan out, your effort has gone to waste. Not only that - you look like hypocrites, for saying one thing and practicing another.

Am I asking your internal communications chief to control the CEO's behavior?

Of course not. That's not realistic, but what IS realistic is to call attention to the gaps between what is said to be valued, and what is actually valued, throughout the organization. Consistency (HR people call it Alignment) is the key.

This is why - speaking of risk-taking - leading the internal communications function is not for the faint of heart. If you lack the guts to tell the emperor when they are naked, you should find another profession.

Here's another example of misalignment in internal communications.

Your company may view itself as fast-paced, team-oriented and customer-focused: nearly every company does.

It only takes one old-school, preachy "don't you dare" memo from HR to blow that perception. The first time your employees read a typical, thoughtless "expense reports filed more than 30 days late will not be processed" bonehead HR memo, your rah-rah internal communications efforts turn to dust.

People aren't stupid. They know where the rubber meets the road.

This is why effective internal communications go stem to stern - from the Podium to the Paystub.

Every communication vehicle, from an all-hands email blast to the CEO's Town Hall meeting, should stem from the same set of goals and values.

It's not hard to meet this goal, once your team is clear on the goal and why you chose it.

It doesn't even require the Messaging Police to review every memo and every page on the company website. It just requires consistent, thoughtful education and awareness-building about the price of off-message communication.

In a typical organization, the biggest trouble spots in Podium to Paystub communication-alignment efforts are IT, Finance, HR and Facilities.

These staff guys have grown up with the idea that they get to set policies and communicate them, period. Having that orientation, these managers might not immediately see how their well-intentioned, kneejerk policy-implementation efforts can derail your carefully honed communications plan.

I worked in one company that preached the virtues of global, 24/7, virtual collaboration.

We're Where You Are, was the message. But one day the Accounting department announced that it expected invoices from all departments to be hand-delivered to Accounting to speed payment. That edict completely undermined the "virtual" theme and was quickly withdrawn. It takes a new mentality - one that the Internal Communications chief can reinforce in every interaction with fellow leaders - to move an organization from disjointed, at-odds communication to a set of aligned voices, singing in harmony.

It's amazing when it happens. Employees begin to believe the messaging, and to incorporate it into their thinking. You'll see the results in customer interactions and in the speed of change efforts. Customers will perceive it. Job candidates and vendors will pick up on it, too. But it's an all-out effort: far past the language in your lovely printed pieces, you've got to touch the paystub, the podium, and everything in between.

TEN UNMISTAKABLE SIGNS OF A FEAR-BASED WORKPLACE

I did not know what a fear-based workplace was the first time I started working in one. At first, I thought the problem was me.

Maybe I didn't have the right clothes or know the right business jargon. I walked on eggshells at work. I went home anxious and discouraged every night.

Gradually it dawned on me that it wasn't just me. My co-workers were uptight, too. No one was having a good time in our workplace. What made everyone so nervous and fearful?

It can take time to realize that you work in a fear-based environment. We can't bear to think that we took a new job in a broken company!

A fear-based workplace is a place where fear is the predominant energy. A healthy workplace is one where trust is the predominant energy.

Trust and fear cannot co-exist in the same place. People who pretend they can co-exist are afraid to admit what their body knows: managerial fear overpowers trust every time.

Either the leaders in an organization trust their employees, or they don't. A fearful CEO will hire yes-men and yes-women to work for them. Anyone with a backbone will not last working for the fearful (and fear-inducing) CEO

Confident leaders trust themselves enough to hire people they can trust.

They don't watch their employees like hawks. They don't enact rules and policies to cover every situation, because they know their employees will rise to every challenge.

They don't set up control mechanisms to keep people from using their native smarts and ingenuity. They don't measure every keystroke and every minute spent on any activity.

They know that focusing on their mission and big, shared goals is a million times more important than measuring everything in sight.

Lots of policies and yardsticks everywhere are unmistakable signs of a fear-based workplace. Measurement of non-essential things is the first sign of a workplace ruled by fear.

Here are 10 more signs:

1. In a fear-based workplace, everyone is focused on their daily goals. They have to be because if they miss a goal, they could lose their job. You won't get collaboration or innovation out of people who are scared to death!

2. In a fear-based culture, managers and HR people specialize in assigning work, measuring results, punishing infractions and maintaining order. In a healthy culture, managers and HR people specialize in listening to employees, problem-solving with them, celebrating successes and envisioning even greater successes!

3. In a fear-based environment, people are afraid to tell the truth because they already know no one wants to hear it. How do they know this? It's obvious, because the biggest truth of all - namely, "Our culture is horrible, but bad things happen to people who say so" is never acknowledged. It is the elephant in the room.

4. In a fear-based company, people talk incessantly about who's up and who's down in the company stock index. The rumor mill is more credible than official communication. In a healthy company, managers and employees talk

about sticky topics. They don't avoid them just because they are awkward to address.

5. In a fear-based company, employees wonder whether they'll still have a job next week. A great performance review or an on-the-job triumph does not guarantee anyone another week of employment. People work under a cloud of fear and suspicion. Managers are afraid to recognize and reinforce their teams, because they might get in trouble for doing so.

6. In a fear-based workplace, following rules and avoiding blame are every team's top priorities. Collaborating, experimenting and having fun do not make the list. If there is a company mission statement on the wall, no one cares about it: the only mission employees can focus on is "Don't screw up!"

7. In a fear-based environment, managers talk about collaboration and out-of-the-box thinking but no one takes them seriously. You cannot get collaboration or new ideas from beaten-down employees.

8. In a fear-based culture, employees disappear without warning. When someone disappears, people speak their names in whispers if they mention them at all.

9. In a fear-based workplace the smartest and most capable employees don't get promoted. The people who get promoted are the ones who most wholeheartedly embrace the fear-based culture.

10. In a fear-based environment, the hardest thing to do is to stay human. When you keep your sense of humor, your warmth and your confidence despite the cloud of fear, you can expect to be labeled 'unprofessional' or worse.

If you work in a fear-based workplace, is there anything you can do about it apart from quitting your job?

You can stand up for yourself and your co-workers but if you do, you have to be ready to get a job fast if you are pushed out the door for naming the elephant.

In a fear-based culture your manager may throw up their hands and say "I agree with the points you're making, but there's nothing I can do to change things! We just have to put up with it and do our best."

Do not get angry with your manager for being so wimpy. Your manager is merely showing you what they are capable of right now.

If you have more confidence than your manager does, that's a sign that you are ready for a big step out of fear and into trust -- and a big step out of your toxic workplace into one that deserves you more!

WHOSE BRAND IS IT, ANYWAY?

"So anyway, that was my old company's policy," said the breathless guy on the phone, whose name turned out to be Phil. "They used to tell us that we could have a LinkedIn profile, but we couldn't use the company's name. Paranoid much?"

"I'm trying to think of a possible rationale for that," I said. "Were they running a Ponzi scheme or something? Was the place a Mafia front?"

"Not as far as I know," said Phil. "It was a logistics and distribution company. They were just afraid of everything, afraid of their employees, afraid of somebody doing or saying something wrong. That's why I quit, in fact. Now, I've got the company name on my LinkedIn profile, of course. How else am I going to account for those four hellish years?"

"So, that was the old company," I said. "What's the story with your new company?"

"I took a new job four months ago," said Phil. "Great people, great company. No problems. A guy I haven't met more than maybe three times just got promoted to VP, and he announced a new policy: no LinkedIn usage will be allowed, at all. Not just at work, I mean - he says we can't have a presence on LinkedIn, period. Afraid of somebody misrepresenting the company somehow, is what I heard."

"Whoa," I said. "That's a new one on me. Total LinkedIn black-out. Who did horrible things to this VP when he was little? The guy sounds like a damaged individual, to be honest with you."

"No doubt," said Phil, "but can they do that? Is it legal?"

"You got me, Phil," I said. "You know I'm not a lawyer. It probably is legal - I mean, you work there by choice - but who wants to work for people like that? You're suddenly supposed to not exist online? What happens to your LinkedIn network? What, you're supposed to kiss it goodbye, with your recommendations and all of your back-and-forth correspondence on LinkedIn and the rest of your LinkedIn archive? Thanks for the decade of online networking, peace out?"

"Evidently," said Phil. "What do you recommend?"

"I'm going to give Mr. Fearful, your VP, the benefit of the doubt and assume he has no idea what he's asking of you guys. It's ridiculous. Would he ask you to also quit your poker club and your church and your gym because you might describe your job or your employer inaccurately? As a matter of fact, they could prohibit you from talking about your job at all, or even confirming that you have a job, because you might say the wrong thing. The guy doesn't realize that he's overstepping wildly. Somebody has to find his voice, or hers, and have a conversation with the gentleman. Why not you?"

The line was silent. "I guess it's either that, or quit tomorrow," said Phil. "It's hard to find a job, but my LinkedIn network is important too." "It's not even that," I added. "It's the presumption, combined with the cluelessness of the request. Your brand is your brand. His brand is his, and the company brand belongs to all of you who work there."

"It's a real thing," said Phil, "This question, 'Who controls my brand?'"

"It's a huge thing!" I agreed with him. "It's a canary in the coal mine issue, too."

"A what, now?" Phil wanted to know. "Canary in the coal mine," I said. "The miners used to bring canaries down into the mines with them, in cages, and if the canary died, the miners knew there was bad stuff in the air, and they had to get out."

"Tough deal for the canary," said Phil.

"And for people like you easing their bosses into the nineteen-nineties, when online branding started to be a thing," I said. "Your boss just got the memo: people are talking about themselves, and they're talking about their jobs in your company."

"I said that your whose-brand-is-it-anyway? question is a canary in the coal mine, because it's a signal that a bigger question is coming right behind. Whose life is it? Whose career path is it? Employers don't offer what they used to offer people — decades of secure employment with great retirement benefits, for instance - so the contract is broken.

It's over.

People aren't going to fork over their brands, their great ideas, every waking hour of their lives, and all their passion — why would they? They're running their own careers. They might not even have chosen to do that, but it's too bad; their companies aren't running their careers in any meaningful way. They'd be crazy not to take matters into their own hands."

"So, in a way it's good this happened," said Phil. "Maybe the universe wants me to bail on this job after four months and go find a better place."

"You know what, Phil," I gently suggested, "I don't think you need to start job-hunting just yet. Your VP is out of it on this LinkedIn issue, but once he comes back to earth things may work out fine. It's not logical, or reasonable, or human or even businesslike to ask hundreds of people to shut down their online branding platforms and networks. I think your poor VP got spooked somehow, maybe reading some random thing an ex-employee wrote on his LinkedIn profile— "

"That's it!" said Phil. "It has to be. There was a guy who worked here with me, we crossed over each other for maybe two months, and it was contentious, and I don't know the details, but the guy left very suddenly."

"Go look at the guy's LinkedIn profile," I said. "Let's say the guy didn't take the company name - your company's name, I mean - off his profile. The VP tells him he has to, the guy says go pound sand. There's your power struggle. VP says, no LinkedIn for anybody!"

"Oh my gosh," said Phil. "That fits. That's got to be the story."

"So, you've got this new VP who has to prove himself, and a difficult guy runs roughshod over his I'm-a-VP-now ego, and he's a little fearful anyway, and the edict comes down. And the guy has not a clue about social networking— "

"No LinkedIn profile, did I mention that?" asked Phil.

"No, but that reinforces the idea that he's behind the curve where LinkedIn is concerned and he's freaked out about that, and now he's a VP and LinkedIn becomes a control thing, and he loses the first round," I went on. "Social media itself becomes the enemy."

"And his way of dealing with it, this idea that people have brands of their own even though they work for him, is to try and stop it," said Phil.

"Good luck to him on that," I said.

"We are in the era of brand collisions.

"Ever do a LinkedIn search on the word 'Enron?' I have thirty thousand LinkedIn connections, and strangely enough not one of them has the word Enron on their LinkedIn profile. Weird, right? Big company, but no one worked there?"

"You're saying that company brands can hurt us as individuals, in our own branding," said Phil.

"For sure, and a company's customer-facing brand is affected by its employer branding, too," I explained.

"Your brand is your brand, and no one else's. Talk to the guy, and say 'I haven't been here long, and we haven't had a chance to talk much. I figured I'd come and talk with you about this policy change, because I had a feeling you hadn't necessarily gotten the best advice on managing 21st-century brand collisions.' That will make him pause for a second."

"I'm going to do it. My confidence is spiking. What do I have to lose?" asked Phil. "The worst he can do is fire me."

"I don't think he will," I said. "There is cluelessness that is evil, but you like these people and have felt good about the energy so far. There is a kind of cluelessness that comes from being really badly advised, or terribly uninformed on a topic — LinkedIn, for instance. I'm guessing your guy is in the uninformed category. You're offering him valuable coaching. Let me know how he responds!"

Phil's confidence spike was rewarded, because the VP immediately reversed the no-LinkedIn-usage policy in a flurry of embarrassed backpedaling email blasts. The incident was forgotten, with one extra silver lining: Phil became the guy's informal social networking mentor.

"What's funny is that I'm 49, and the VP is 42," said Phil a few weeks later.

"He can take advice from you," I said. "He might be spooked by a Gen Y teammate coaching him on online branding."

"Thanks for the good counsel," said Phil. "Find your voice, isn't that what you always say?"

"That, and focus on the energy," I said. "Do that, and the branding will take care of itself."

BURN THE EMPLOYEE HANDBOOK AND START OVER

I collect Employee Handbooks for fun because they are so horrifying. I have about fifty of them. They come from large and small companies. They spring from the hard drives of law firms who charge a bundle to write Employee Handbooks for their clients using the same zombified language you could download from any HR website for free.

Nothing has changed in the Employee Handbook world since I was born, over fifty years ago.

We are told that Employee Handbooks must read like crusty, abstruse government manuals because that's what the law requires, but like most of the justifications we hear for trapped-in-amber workplace practices, it isn't true.

There is no legal requirement to write the dreck that fills the typical Employee Handbook. Employers have to follow the laws, of course, but the grotesque, impenetrable legalese is just the way lawyers write. They are writing to protect the employer from its own employees. That's pretty dang sad, and it also doesn't work.

If your company gets sued and the case revolves around the Employee Handbook you had better hope I do not walk into the room as the expert witness for the complainant. I will feel empathy for you in that situation, but the learning will be powerful.

I will point out that at New Employee Orientation, the plaintiff and his or her fellow employees were given two hundred pages of text between the Employee Handbook and a gazillion other documents, and yet were required to sign their names saying that they had received and read the Handbook, understood it and agreed to follow every word in it.

They could not have possibly have read the thing or even opened it then and there in the Orientation meeting and you know it, so the signature page sitting in the employee's personnel file does not get your company off the hook.

After the new-employee orientation meeting the Handbook was never referenced again during the unhappy employee's tenure.

Now that the employee is taking you to court, you pull out the signature form and say that the plaintiff totally understood and agreed with the mountain of sludge crammed between the pages of the handbook.

Whatever the item your employee overlooked or neglected, buried in the handbook as it was, you will have a very tough proving that he or she could or should have known about it, much less interpreted its meaning.

You will have to explain why you communicate with your customers in the simplest and clearest way while you chose 19th-century language for the only document provided to your employees to understand their obligations and yours.

That's a fail.

You will write a big check to the plaintiff. We can't rest on our inhumanly written Employee Handbooks to defend us anymore. There is an increasing expectation that we play fair with our employees, and the language in the standard Employee Handbook is anything but fair to a person who is not a lawyer or a legislator him- or herself.

We are in the age of human communication. We know how people take in information and integrate it. We know the power of images and color and a human voice. We use these things when we communicate with people we value more than we do our employees, like our customers and partners.

Employee Handbooks are stuck in the past. They are not only a waste of time and a weak defense against the sort of employment-law claims I referred to above, but also insulting and off-putting to your teammates.

If you have one shot to give your employees a book about their relationships with your firm, why would you fill that book with obnoxious "You'd better not even think about it!" warnings?

The 50 handbooks I own are full of warnings. Some of them list forty things you can do to get fired, like smacking someone or stealing paperclips. Why don't they go whole hog and list everything you could do to get fired? Then the Employee Handbook would be infinitely long. We'd never finish writing it.

We could get creative. We'll make sure to include that you can get fired for speaking only Klingon at work or hopping from office to office on one foot. If this idea sounds ridiculous, back up one step and you will see that the entire notion of listings "Ways to get fired" in an Employee Handbook is stupid and childish.

The reason Employee Handbooks are so vile is that they come from an era when employees wouldn't care about or react to ugly, us-versus-them language in an official company document.

The employment deal was much better for employees back then than it is now. Back in the Camelot days people would put up with a lot more ridiculousness from their employers than they will now. That makes sense, because their loyalty to the employer was much stronger and the reverse was also true.

Now people are waking up. They ask their managers and HR people "Why is the Employee Handbook written as though the company doesn't trust us? I mean -- you hired us!"

I don't want you to revise your Employee Handbook. As a cultural vehicle -- and that, of course, is what an Employee Handbook is -- the traditional Employee Handbook format and framework are too far gone. Your best bet is to throw out your Employee Handbook or burn it and start over.

Your CEO can address your employees in the first page or two, then turn over the mic to someone else. That person doesn't have to be the head of HR. Your front-desk receptionist could have the mic and be the voice of your Employee Handbook. You could pass the mic around in your handbook and let different employees write different sections.

You have to shift the frame in your Handbook from "Don't you dare misbehave!" to "Here's what we think you will find helpful as a new employee here."

One person can talk about the dress code -- not spelled out in fussy stitch-level detail that insults the talented and capable-of-self-dressing people you employ, but in general terms that honor the people you chose to carry your flag. Another voice can talk about the company's commitment to equal employment opportunity.

Most Employee Handbooks are accusatory. They come from the same place as the sign posted in the fitting rooms of low-end department stores: "Shoplifters Will Be Prosecuted." Nice message to take in while I'm trying on jeans!

The Employee Handbook needs to go in the opposite direction, talking about your commitment to non-criminals rather than your threats toward the bad guys.

The rest of the Employee Handbook -- maybe 25 pages total, no more -- will provide the workplace equivalent of the book you find on the desk in a hotel room. That's what a handbook is -- a guide to navigating in a new place.

There won't be any threats in it. There won't be any talking-down-from-the-sky language and there won't be any governmental garbage language to wade through. Your new Employee Handbook will be a guide to help a newbie employee understand your shop. It will be readable and friendly and warm.

What a relief that will be to your employees! You can use your new Employee Handbook, the one with a human voice, as a recruiting tool and a training tool. You can point to it proudly and every time you update it, you can add something fun and clever to it, like a crossword puzzle or doodle frames. You can have fun with it.

We are in a new era. We are building a healthier workplace together.

Tell your employment lawyers to back off and let you write the Employee Handbook your employees want to read. You can enlist creative people from around your company to collaborate with you on the project.

You can grow your team's trust level and replace your tired, old-school Employee Handbook at the same time!

THE FIVE MOST COMMON CULTURE PROBLEMS -- AND THEIR SOLUTIONS

Dear Liz,

I'm interviewing to become the first HR Director for a business-to-business services firm. I've had two interviews and I really like what I've heard so far. For my third (and I believe, final) interview, the regional President who will interview me has asked me to prepare questions for him.

I do have questions for him, but I want to focus in on his Business Pain as I've learned from you to do! If they didn't have significant pain, they wouldn't be replacing their former HR Manager (who moved out of state) with an HR Director now.

The company outsources its payroll, benefits and HRIS to a third-party vendor. Everyone I have met in the company says that the vendor does a great job. So, I think the region's Business Pain is more in the area of culture, which is not surprising because they are growing fast and hiring a lot of people.

What are some of the most common culture problems you observe, and if you can share them in a few words, how do you solve the most common problems? I want to talk about my experience creating training programs, communication programs and retention programs as I think these kinds of interventions could be very useful for my (hopefully) new employer.

Thanks Liz!

Yours,
Chris

Dear Chris,

Often as HR practitioners we are taught to see the world through program-colored glasses. That is, we get used to observing a team and a workplace with the question, "What do these folks need -- more training, more communication or a different pay structure?" planted in our heads.

We have tools at our disposal -- the ability to write policies, classrooms and devices through which we can reach our teammates, and so on -- and we want to use them! When we think about ways to help our employer thrive, we often think about designing something, implementing something or measuring something.

I teach the opposite approach. Forget about interventions for now and focus on what is happening inside your possible next employer. What is causing your regional President sleepless nights right now? I guarantee you he isn't lying awake thinking "I need a new leadership development program!"

Pain shows up in little ways at first. Your regional President (I'm calling him Mike) undoubtedly runs into daily or many-times-daily issues that make him wonder "Are we doing everything we need to do to keep this team focused and connected as we grow?" The answer may well be "No." It's very hard for growing companies to keep all the pieces together.

Small companies tend to grow a ton in a short term and then overreact by installing too much HR infrastructure (and the worst, crusty kind of infrastructure to boot). They rush to install formal systems like 360-degree feedback programs and annual Employee Engagement Surveys.

Try to resist the urge to suggest even more weenie programs to Mike when you meet him. Listen to him and anticipate his problems, instead. That's how you will grow your Pain-Spotting muscles!

It's tempting to go straight to solutions, but I don't recommend that you do that. The only way you will build trust and credibility with Mike is by truly hearing him and probing more and more deeply for his most pressing Business Pain. Once you have a good sense of Mike's pain, you can tell stories about times when you dealt with similar types of pain.

These are called Dragon-Slaying Stories!

Here are the five most common corporate culture problems I see, and ideas for solving them.

1. **Employees are bored, discouraged and/or generally unhappy.** You'll know your prospective teammates are less than excited because Mike or another interviewer will tell you about it, because you spot it with your own eyes when you're in the facility or because Mike talks to you about quality control or attendance issues. How do you solve this? You can't force people to be happy. You have to listen to them, and you can't even do that until you build trust with them. That's a slow, gradual process but it's worth the effort!

2. **Supervisors are under-equipped, so they over-supervise**. Naturally a new supervisor thrown into the deep end of the pool will feel anxious. Insecure supervisors will often over-manage and get bossy. That will rankle the employees and the negative cycle is reinforced. Before you think about supervisory training, you've got to open lines of communication. You've got to define a supervisor's job for the benefit of everyone -- not just the supervisors -- and then coach and support your supervisors as they grow into the role.

3. **Turnover is too high.** If people are leaving your company regularly to get better jobs and it isn't in your business

plan to employ a revolving door of short timers, you have a turnover problem and thus a culture problem.

The solution is once again to back off on rules and policies and give your employees a voice. It's amazing how people will join in and make great suggestions if only they are respected for what they know and what they bring to the organization.

Turnover problems are closely related to the predominant leadership style in your organization. Many if not most supervisors believe their number one priority is to keep employees in line. That approach will drive talented people out the door faster than you can replace them. If you're not already teaching, reinforcing and modeling trust-based leadership, now is a great time to start.

4. **Conflict or tension is palpable.** The easiest culture problem for a leader or a whole leadership team to overlook is a dark, heavy feeling in the air. Nobody talks about it because they are afraid to bring up the topic "Why is it so hard to work here?"

   No one wants to be the bearer of bad news, but all the employees know that it feels like death to walk into work every day. The solution here is that you will be the truth-teller, and if you're not willing to do that, don't take the job! You have an advantage over the managers who got there before you. You were hired to build a healthy culture. That's what HR Directors do!

5. **Communication only flows down, and not up.** A sure sign of an unhealthy culture is communication that flows down rather than up and across. Some companies put out memos and across-the-board email blasts to communicate with their employees, but the executives and managers don't stop and talk with employees when they run into them. In a healthy company, everybody is always talking.

Managers are always asking, "What do you think about that? Is it a good idea? How would you do it differently?" They want to hear people's opinions, no matter what they are. You can instill this kind of communication once you get the job -- and you can probe for this kind of pain on your interview.

You can start your Pain-Spotting conversation by asking your possible next boss, "In the midst of all this growth, I'd have to imagine that you sometimes run into communication roadblocks and disturbances in the force. Sometimes it's absenteeism and other times supervisors aren't sure how to manage their teams, for instance. Have you been running into these kinds of issues?"

You are becoming a champion at probing for Business Pain and seeing any prospective employer through a cultural lens rather than a break/fix lens. This is a big step in your evolution as an HR Minister of Culture.

Enjoy the journey!

Yours,
Liz

WHY PLEASING YOUR BOSS SHOULD BE YOUR LOWEST PRIORITY

We are stepping out of one working world and into a new one. Most working people are slow to make the change. We can't see that the glacier is melting under our feet. Forty years ago, when you took a new job, you could reasonably expect to stay there for five or 10 years.

Now you can't. We are always in job-hunting or semi-job-hunting mode. We can't go to sleep on our careers and pretend that because we have a job right now, our careers are in fine shape.

It used to be that your boss made all the important career decisions for you. Your boss decided when you got promoted and what kind of raise you were eligible for at your annual review. Your manager still makes those decisions, but promotions are few and far between and your raise cannot possibly keep up with the real value of your work.

Those two decisions -- who gets promoted, when, and who gets a 2% versus a 5% raise -- are much less significant to your career arc now than they were in the days of lifelong employment with one firm. They don't matter a lot, but your ability to get hired whenever you need to matters tremendously.

Salary compression keeps working people at artificially depressed salary levels. They earn less money staying with one employer than they would earn if they changed jobs more often.

For years working people have accepted that trade-off (compressed salaries versus the stability of a long-term job) because we crave job security. We assume that sticking with one employer for years on end will buy us something valuable -- chips that will help us if the company should announce headcount reductions, for instance.

We are wrong in that assumption.

It's hard for us to grasp that there is no job security anymore. There is no employer than can promise to keep you employed for a long time, or for any particular length of time.

Our job security is something we build in ourselves these days. We carry it around with us. There is only one way for us to build security for ourselves, and that is to stay marketable. The person with the most job security is anybody who knows that if their current job should disappear, there are a lot of other places they could find work.

That's the person who doesn't worry about pleasing the boss just because people have been pleasing bosses for 200 years. Our sound sleeper isn't trying to get fired, but if he or she gets fired, life goes on! They already know they're employable somewhere else. (Do you?)

You stay marketable when your resume and your confidence are constantly growing. You stay marketable when you're always learning.

Pleasing your boss at work is your lowest priority these days, because pleasing your boss cannot move your career forward in the way that managing your own path can. Your boss' power to move you ahead in most companies is far weaker than your own power to take your career wherever you want it to go.

It's true that your boss can dismiss you if they want to, but you cannot live your life in fear of another person's emotions. It makes no sense, for instance, to give up your personal life for the job when you could be out of a job for almost any reason in the blink of an eye no matter what sacrifices you've made.

You have to do your job well enough to keep the job. Beyond that, it's not a good investment of your energy and attention to strive to be your boss's favorite employee or to win a gold star or the maximum annual pay increase. It's more important to keep an eye on the world outside your office walls and to keep your resume growing.

It's astonishing to me how much faith working people put in their boss's loyalties when your boss makes you no guarantees whatsoever about continued employment, even if you bend to his or her every whim.

We met a lady named Rupa. She said, "I spent the last six months working on a huge project for my VP, and then I got laid off. I worked nights and weekends. I killed myself on that project, and then I lost my job."

"Why was the project important to your company?" we asked. "How did your work help your employer win in its marketplace?"

"I have no idea," said Rupa. "I was given the project to do and I did it."

We helped Rupa retrace her steps and figure out why her biggest project was her boss's biggest priority, too. Nowadays, we have to complete that exercise in real time – to understand the impact of our actions while we are engaged in them.

We can't take a passive view of our work anymore.

The rug could be pulled out from under you at any moment and if that happens, you have to be ready to talk about the contribution you made to each employer you worked for.

You have to see how your work directly impacts your employer's goals. We are all analysts now. We have to get altitude on our work and see how our work makes our employers money. That's how we'll snag our next engagement!

You can't afford to worry about pleasing your manager. In the end, it doesn't matter if your manager likes your work -- it only matters that he or she needs you on the team. Your focus must be on what your manager *needs* to run the department and your ability to meet those needs -- not your manager's personal likes and dislikes or shifting priorities.

The older we get, the easier it becomes to stop worrying about pleasing your manager every time he or she has a request, and to focus more on staying tuned in to the way your work helps your department hit its goals. When you know that you perform work your employer desperately needs and that not a lot of people can do, you gain a huge amount of power.

People are fickle, and managers are fickler than most. We advise our clients to treat every job as a consulting gig and like any consulting engagement, to know at the outset what a successful project conclusion looks like.

Who could sleep at night knowing that they keep their job only because they please their manager -- not because their work contributes in a fundamental way to their employer's results? That person is at risk of getting the boot the first time the manager wakes up in a bad mood and wants to save some money by slashing headcount.

I don't want you to go to work and spend your energy trying to make your manager happy. I'd rather have you sleep soundly on your pillow because you know that your manager couldn't replace you easily and couldn't duplicate your subject-matter expertise without a lot of hassle.

That is a useful kind of leverage. It gives you power in the hiring equation -- not just for the manager you have now, but as long as your career continues.

We are all business owners now. Pleasing the boss is the booby prize in the new-millennium workplace. Let the boss get his or her pleasure somewhere else -- you focus on your own path, your own goals and your value to this employer and every employer down the line.

TEN COOL BENEFITS TO OFFER YOUR EMPLOYEES

Dear Liz,

I am a follower of yours and a new HR manager! I have been in HR for three and a half years, doing a mix of things from recruiting to employee relations to benefits and compensation. Now I am the HR manager in a small company. I have a small budget to work with and I'd like to add some fun elements and benefits if I can.

Do you have a list of good, inexpensive programs I can offer to our employees to help make our workplace more fun and to show our appreciation?

Thanks!

Yours,
Bryce

Dear Bryce,

Congratulations on your new position! That is exciting. I will share a list of cool employee programs with you, but I must clear up one thing first.

The fun ideas that I will list in a moment will not make your workplace cooler or more human unless it is already cool and human. As an HR Manager you are helping to bake a cake. Fun programs and perks are the icing on the cake. The actual cake is a million times more important than the icing.

If your workplace is open and honest, you've got a good, healthy cake. If you trust the people you hire enough to let them do their jobs without hindering them at every moment with pointless rules and yardsticks, then your cake is solid. If your workplace is fear-filled and toxic, then the fanciest icing in the world can't help you.

Your highest priority as an HR Manager is to manage the trust level in your company by telling the truth about everything that happens and encouraging other people to do the same thing. Tear down any stupid bureaucratic systems that spring up and address any conflicts that arise right away.

Ask your employees how they're doing (not how they're doing on their goals -- how they're doing as people) and listen to their answers. Replace the Employee Engagement Survey with lots of open conversation and teach your fellow managers to do the same thing.

Tell your CEO the truth about what customers, employees, vendors and the general public are saying and thinking about your company and push for the human answer to every question, because it will always be the right business answer in the long run.

Make your recruiting process fast, warm and human. Then you'll have a tasty cake to decorate! Here are the ten cool benefits I promised you:

1. Call your local restaurants and hit them up for coupons for your employees, or a discount that your employees will receive when they eat in the restaurants and show their ID badges. This works especially well if you also remember to patronize the same restaurants for your catered lunches!

2. Call your local oil-change service providers and arrange for them to send out a truck one day so that your employees can get their oil changed in your parking lot while they're inside working. Do a lot of internal marketing so

that your first oil-change event is well attended, and your oil change provider will be happy to send a truck out on a regular basis.

3. Organize a blood drive. (That's a benefit?) It's a benefit if people want to donate blood anyway and you make it easy for them by hosting the blood drive right in your building. You and your fellow HR folks and/or managers will stick around and chit-chat with the blood donors and introduce them to one another. Building community at work is a great way to raise your organization's trust level and help people connect across departments. Your company will provide the snacks and drinks for blood donors and volunteers!

4. Set up a series of brown-bag lunch lectures and performances delivered by your employees with special interests and talents to your other employees who are interested in the topics. You can spring for the drinks and dessert if you like.

5. Create a simple internal discussion community where your employees can get advice and tips from one another, give away baby clothes and other items they don't need and generally support and learn from one another.

6. Invite your local credit union(s) to share their offerings with your employees. Credit unions are awesome and have tons of programs that can benefit your team members.

7. Set up a new-employee buddy program where each new employee is paired up with a longer-term employee who works in a different department. You can authorize the new employee's buddy to take the new employee to lunch one day during his or her first week of work. The buddy in another department can make introductions and check in on the newcomer a few times during his or her first few

weeks. It's fun to be a buddy and fun to have one to help you get comfortable in a new workplace!

8. Experiment with flexibility in starting and ending time and working from home in whatever ways work best for your organization. Take slow steps and make sure that everyone knows you're in pilot mode—trying new things out to see how well they work. Your ability to offer even a little flexibility can make a huge difference in your ability to hire and keep great people.

9. Call your local museums and cultural institutions along with movie theaters, amusement parks and other attractions, and ask them about employee discount days, as many institutions offer them. The first step is to ask!

10. Where will you find the time to make these phone calls and email overtures? You will have more time when you get out of Compliance Mode (also known as Playing HR Defense) and into Culture-Building Mode (playing HR Offense—a much more exciting and influential game)!

Outsource the "quant" side of your job to one of the very capable vendors who specialize in taking on the number-crunching and record-keeping aspects of the HR function. You are the Minister of Culture, and your job is to make your workplace a wonderful place to work!

All the best to you Bryce -
Liz

'MY VP OF CULTURE DESTROYED MY COMPANY'S CULTURE'

Dear Liz,

I am proud of the company I built but I have never felt all that comfortable in the 'people' department. The first few employees in our company were high school friends of mine and most of them are still here. Now we have 280 employees.

I had a part-time HR person, Sylvia, who took care of payroll and benefits for our first few years. As we grew bigger, I thought about hiring a full-time HR person, but things were going pretty smoothly and I had a lot of other priorities, so I didn't do it. We have used an HR consultant, Barry, several times for projects and he has helped us a lot.

Earlier this year I got some feedback from my management team and one of our Board members that the company is big enough to keep a full-time HR Manager or Director busy. Ironically the woman I hired, "Maggie," required that her title be VP of Culture, and I agreed with that because I didn't think it made any difference one way or the other.

Her salary was in line with what I was willing to pay so we made a deal.

She came with great credentials. She lasted six months. Now I am undoing the damage Maggie did to our company.

I got snowed by Maggie's argument that our company needed all new HR systems, policies and procedures. She came in here six months ago and basically got everybody upset right away by writing new policies and clamping down on our formerly pretty casual culture, starting with our dress code.

You may wonder why I went along with Maggie's ideas. I thought that she knew more about the field of HR than I did and of course I wanted to support a new member of my leadership team.

I trust our employees very much. A lot of them have been here for years. When a plant foreman, Peter, came to see me to say that he was about ready to quit over his disagreements with Maggie, I finally got the message. I called a meeting and our management team, including Maggie and me, aired the topic of our culture and our HR systems.

It was a difficult meeting but at the end of it Maggie said, "I don't think your company is ready to step up to the next level" and she gave notice. That was fantastic because I didn't have to fire her.

Now employees are lining up to tell me and the other managers how much they hate the new "culture" that Maggie installed. We are undoing the damage bit by bit. I would like to say that I've learned a powerful lesson except I have no idea what the lesson is.

I am completely gun-shy about hiring a new HR leader, although we have a lot of hiring to do and I'm sure we could make good use of a more people-friendly HR manager. What do you recommend?

Thanks,

Dear Mark,

Many entrepreneurs and other leaders have been bitten by the same snake that got you. They are more removed from the HR function than from other functions, and they don't trust their sturdy instincts. They think that the leadership of HR requires different muscles than the ones that the heads of other functions bring to the job. That's false!

An HR leader looks out for the culture of the company, not by clamping down and destroying the trust you've built up but by celebrating it and spreading the goodwill around. There are HR laws and regulations that must be complied with of course, but in a healthy culture you run very little risk of breaking any employment laws.

Healthy organizations play way out in front of the net, you might say. They don't focus on merely complying with the minimum requirements of employment laws. You wouldn't treat your customers only as well as the law requires, would you? You treat your customers like gold!

The right HR leader will help you and your leaders remember and give weight to the human aspect of every business decision, from a re-organization to a change in the health plan.

When you as a busy CEO or any of your leaders forgets the human perspective, your HR leader will bring that topic back to the forefront. Your CFO looks out for the long-term and short-term financial health of your business. You can't be thinking about the financial impact of every decision at every moment, so your CFO does that for you.

Your HR leader does the same thing, except that their priority is the trust level in the organization rather than dollars and cents. Ironically, your HR leader should be the Minister of Culture in your company, but merely sticking a VP of Culture title on a person like Maggie will not change their underlying worldview.

The next time you hire an HR chief, involve your managers and the staff members you trust to safeguard your friendly culture as your company grows. There is nothing more important in your business plan than that. It's great that you took Peter's feedback seriously and organized the meeting that led to Maggie's resignation.

I'm certain that you have already gained trust points with your team for engineering her departure, although you have more work to do as you restore the trust that Maggie's short and destructive reign weakened for your teammates.

This would be a great time to host a Town Hall Meeting. You can thank your team for keeping you posted on their observations and reactions to things going on at work and let them know that you're looking for a new HR leader to replace Maggie. Ask them what they want in an HR chief.

Don't disparage Maggie of course, but open the door wide to any feedback your teammates might want to give you in the moment or later, in a more private way. More importantly, don't ever believe that somebody's HR credentials trump your own gut feelings about the people in your company. You wouldn't have gotten this far ignoring your gut in any other realm -- don't do it in the HR arena, either!

All the best,
Liz

TEN TOXIC BELIEFS THAT KEEP HR IN THE DARK AGES

You wouldn't think someone who writes and speaks about the workplace would get hate mail, but then again, a lot of people are mired in fear. When you tell them what they don't want to hear, they can react strongly!

When I write a story telling jobseekers that they don't have to give up their salary history, angry old-school, blarney-and-bluster-style recruiters come out of the woodwork.

"Great way to get people blacklisted by recruiters like me!" they write, totally confirming my intuition that bullying by recruiters is a more common feature of the modern job hunt than most people realize.

HR people show up in my inbox with an eighty/twenty ratio of fans and haters. What's to hate in my HR advice? For starters, I tell HR people that their job is to be Minister of Culture in their organizations, not policy-writers or police officers.

Some HR folks don't like the new vision for HR. They are more comfortable keeping tabs on employees and writing them up for small infractions.

The world is changing fast. Already the most marketable people won't stand still to be treated like children or criminals. They'll be gone. Some employers got that memo a long time ago. They treat their employees and job applicants like gold.

Some employers are stuck in a time warp. They don't realize that their reputations precede them. Good employees won't even consider working for them.

Here in Colorado there is a list of about fifteen large employers that no self-respecting jobseeker would ever work for. They'll take bit lower pay or stick to independent consulting rather than go to work in one of these sweatshops.

All fifteen are large employers whose names you know. How can these organizations not be aware that the most talented people in the state are staying away from them in droves? Maybe they are aware, but they don't care. In a fear-filled organization, people with self-esteem wouldn't stick around anyway. They'd be fired or quit within a few months, because the atmosphere is so oppressive.

I always wonder why the Boards of Directors at these organizations are so asleep at the wheel when it comes to corporate culture. Any message board would tell a curious Board member (or shareholder, for that matter) that the company they help to lead or own a piece of is broken. Money is being wasted - very large sums -- but the hateful policies and bring-the-hammer-down leadership style persists.

Here are ten beliefs that I run into very often in organizations who haven't connected the dots yet to see that when people are set free to do great things, great things will result. If the HR folks in your organization spout this nonsense, you can try to educate them, or you can get your resume on the street and head for higher ground.

1. Everyone is easily replaceable. If you don't like it here, we'll find someone who will.

2. Your manager is an authority figure, and you are not. Your job is to do what you're told.

3. We create these policies for a reason. It's none of your business what that reason is.

4. Our mission in HR is to keep the company out of court. We are on the company's side, not yours (and yes, there are sides)!

5. Someone higher in the organization than you has already settled that issue. It is not up for discussion.

6. If we make an exception for you, we have to do it for everyone.

7. Your job description and pay grade define you. If you have talents that aren't specified in the job description, don't expect to be paid for them.

8. Don't spread your ideas around the company. Your manager will tell you what to do. It's not your job to tell people what you think.

9. While you are here in this building, you're on company time. Don't engage in small talk here or take care of personal business. You can do that after hours -- unless we tell you to stay late to work on a project or send you home with work, or email you or text you, or call you.

10. We will let you know when you screwed up. When you do your job, we won't say anything about it, because that's what you're paid for.

These beliefs are pretty common. They all spring from fear -- fear that we might not retain control (whatever that means) if we soften and become human at work. People in fear put up walls and work hard to let you know that they're in charge and you are not.

Fear in organization is a sickness. The best thing to do when you run into organizational fear is to name it. You can say "It sure seems like a lot of people are scared to death around here. Can we talk about that?"

If you feel afraid to do that, then you are in fear yourself. Toxic cultures retain their stranglehold on the hearts and brains of employees by staying unaddressed and unmentioned. If you want to reclaim your power, speak up about the quality of the air in your workplace.

Say something to another employee. You will find that you're not the only one who feels the way you do. We are all growing muscles together. As the flower children in the sixties used to say, "If you're not part of the solution, you're part of the problem."

The road to a healthy, switched-on workplace is right in front of us. To build the trust level in your company and reduce the fear, all you need to do is talk about those things. How magical is that?

FIVE REASONS FEAR-BASED MANAGEMENT IS THE ONLY KIND WE KNOW

Everybody likes the sound of the word 'trust,' but putting trust-based leadership into action takes patience and humility, and these are not typically virtues we honor in the business world. Replacing fear with trust requires us to look at our words and behaviors critically, and that is not something emphasized in our never-ending conversations about KPIs and quarterly goals.

Speed and decisive action, however, are right up our alley! Even managers who want to cultivate trust-based leadership abilities have to take baby steps at first, because trust-based leadership concepts are foreign to them. Why is that? Why is fear-based management the only kind of management most of us are familiar with? Here are five reasons!

We grew up being managed through fear ourselves.

Most of us were raised by fear-based authority figures at school. We grew up afraid to get in trouble, and we know how to get along in that system. It is familiar to us. Managers who want to cultivate trust-based leadership in their teams may run into opposition from their own managers, who tell them "Toughen up and manage your team, instead of letting them manage you!"

Nobody wants to seem weak. We have twisted reality around to convince ourselves that people who manage through fear are tough, whereas in reality, trust-based leaders are tough and fear-based managers are weak. Fearful managers only have one tool to use in every managerial situation, and that tool is a threat of consequences or even termination if a team member doesn't do their bidding.

What's tough about that? Their authority is fake. It was bestowed on them by somebody else. Trust-based leaders inspire trust through their words and actions. They don't stoop to picking up a hammer every time they need to get something done through other people.

Any bully on the street can threaten people. Trust-based leaders don't use threats. They trust themselves and the people they supervise enough to work things out without threats of disciplinary action or termination. It takes a strong person to be human, but that is not the traditional management style our executive leaders know!

Our culture reinforces fear-based management.

I live in the United States, whose first European settlers (apart from the Vikings) were religious fanatics, if we are honest. We learn in school that the Puritans came to New England to escape religious persecution, but the minute they got there they became very comfortable persecuting other people for their religious views. There is a statue in downtown Boston of Mary Dyer, who was killed because she refused to give up her Quaker faith. How awful do you have to be to kill a Quaker?

We grew up with the Puritan ideas that sparing the rod spoils the child, that we must be broken upon the rock and that the only honorable way to live is to spend our lives correcting our defects and atoning for our sins. You can see how this cultural frame fits nicely into the fear-based leadership worldview. It's only a small step to managing people the same way in the workplace -- through fear and control, that is.

We grow up with the idea that authority and punishment go hand in hand.

We heard from our client Greg, who had been to a leadership training workshop at his company. "This sounds weird to me," he said. "Does this sound weird to you guys?" Greg read to us from a handbook he had been given at his leadership training workshop. The handbook included this message that a new supervisor was encouraged to share with his or her new teammates:

We both have a job to do, and as long as you do your job, you'll be fine with me. I have standards and policies that I will explain to you, and I am happy to answer your questions. I want to be fair and reasonable with you, and all I ask is that you give me your best work every day. Do that, and we won't have any problems.

That sounded weird to us, the same way it did to Greg. The new manager is telling his or her teammates how to stay on his or her good side but doesn't say a word about his or her intention to support them or serve them in any way.

The new manager only says, "Do your best at work." He or she doesn't say "This job has to grow your flame. I want to know how I can help you. Nothing good or worthy that might happen in this department will happen on its own, without your amazing contribution. I want to help take away any roadblocks that keep you from loving your job."

I'm not sure our Puritan forebear Cotton Mather, who presided over the Salem Witch Trials, would have been able to choke those words out, but the rest of us can send that message easily! We only have to notice how big a step we take out of our cultural frame when we step into trust-based leadership.

Trust-based leadership requires introspection, something most of us haven't practiced before.

Trust-based leadership is personal. As a trusting leader you tell your-self and your teammates "I don't have all the answers. I'm figuring out my job the same way everybody is. We'll all learn together." Introspection means looking inward and taking responsibility for the things we do and say, whether we're proud of them or not.

Traditional leadership training has not emphasized self-reflection, and that's a pity. Self-reflection is a fantastic way to learn!

The costs of fear-based management can be hard to spot and hard to measure.

Fear in a workplace kills the culture and makes companies go bankrupt, but it isn't something that shows up on a balance sheet or an income statement, at least not right away. When fear grips a culture, the best people leave first, but the fear in the environment keeps the higher-ups from acknowledging that they have a problem. If they admitted they had a problem, they'd have to look in the mirror, and that's the one thing they can't do.

More people start to leave, and it becomes harder to hire good people. Customers get the memo and leave for other vendors. The slow cycle downhill is an old and oft-repeated story. Nobody -- not even the Board members charged with keeping the company healthy -- tells the truth, and another firm bites the dust. Fear is a powerful silencer!

Fear-based management is fast, and businesses love speed

Once when I was 21, I went to my then-boyfriend's parents' house to visit. As we entered the house, my boyfriend's dad was yelling at my boyfriend's younger sister, who was about seventeen. All of a sudden, the dad slapped the girl across the face. I remember standing stock still in shock as my boyfriend's sister ran out the front door.

I had not yet been introduced to the dad, who turned to me and said, "You have a problem with corporal punishment?" I was frozen. I couldn't speak. "Well, it's expedient," he said, and walked out of the room. My boyfriend and I didn't stay long and thankfully the abuser's daughter got out of that house herself soon after.

The abusive dad was right -- fear and control are expedient. That's one reason we don't question their value, even in 2016 when we should know better.

Fear makes people bend to our will and keeps us from looking more closely into problems that we don't care to examine. We can simply tell the people in our departments to shut up and do their work and delude ourselves that we are excellent managers.

We can maintain the fiction that being the manager makes us right, automatically. We can pretend that we have nothing to learn from our teammates. We can convince ourselves that as long as we churn out the work on schedule, we have nothing to worry about.

Our teammates know that's not true, and our bodies know it, too. We can pretend that managing through threats and punishments is appropriate in the new-millennium workplace. We can stick our fingers in our ears and take our leadership guidance from seventeenth-century zealots and say inane things like "As a manager, I'm tough but fair."

We can lie to ourselves, or we can step into our power, grow new muscles and speak with our own voice. It's our choice. It's your choice, every minute of every day. What will your choice be today?

TEN REASONS OUT-OF-THE-BOX THINKERS ARE UNHAPPY EMPLOYEES

It's not easy being a creative thinker in the typical corporate or institutional workplace. It can be hellish, in fact! Managers say, "I want out-of-the-box ideas!" but they don't always mean it. When you show up with new ideas and new perspectives, managers can get threatened very easily. Your fellow employees can get threatened, too.

I was taught to shut my mouth and do what I was told as a very young child and you probably were, too. All the way back in first grade I got the message that I was a troublemaker only because I said something in class that the teacher wasn't expecting to hear. Lots of us grow up thinking that people in authority know more than we do, but that is often not the case.

When you get into the working world you will see that a lot of people are asleep at the wheel! They don't think about much. They do their job the way it was explained to them and that's it. They don't ask questions. They don't ponder opportunities. They do exactly what they're told, and they want you to do the same thing!

Here are 10 reasons it can be very difficult for a non-traditional or non-linear-thinking person to work in a corporate or institutional job, or a not-for-profit or startup job or any job.

1. Many managers say, "I want to hear your out-of-the-box ideas!" but they don't want to listen. They are living inside a tiny mental box of their own. They don't necessarily want to be nudged or shoved out of their mental box, least of all by someone who works under them!

2. Organizations are built around formal processes and structures. Your out-of-the-box ideas may threaten those structures and processes or make them obsolete. Maybe your big idea is good for the corporation overall, but that doesn't mean it will be good for the middle managers whose roles and authority your good idea may threaten! Guess what will happen to your good idea when people above you figure out that the implementation of your idea could put them at risk?

3. Organizations of all sizes have currents of fear and trust running through them. Those currents are seldom if ever discussed, but they have huge impact on the organization's ability to succeed. When you propose something out of the norm, you may unintentionally cause the fear level in your organization to spike. Nothing productive can happen when people are in fear. You can tone down your sales approach and try to be content with tiny, incremental changes, but your body may protest. You will not be happy in a place that dims your flame.

4. Many managers hesitate to try new things even in their own departments because they are afraid of getting in trouble if the new idea doesn't pan out. Many organizations large and small still follow procedures that were conceived and written in the 1990s, when business and life were totally different than they are now.

5. Lots of people are overwhelmed at work. They feel that their brain cannot hold one even one more thought -- even a fantastic, breakthrough idea. They are simply out

of bandwidth and you are wasting your time trying to get them to think creatively with you.

6. When you propose idea after idea and each one is shot down, of course your self-esteem plummets. Of course, you get frustrated. You have a brain and you want to use it!

7. Corporations and institutions are linear, boxy things. They are set up like nested sets of boxes. Everybody has a job description and every job description has constraints and limits. Everybody has a boss. Everything is neat and tidy, but only as long as nobody disrupts the system. Interestingly, the real world is always in flux. It's only inside of our organizations that we can delude ourselves, for a little while at least, that things can stay the same and everything will be fine. Anybody with a creative spirit will be frustrated eventually in a boxed-up, unchanging organization where uniformity is valued over brilliance!

8. It is frustrating to be stalled at every turn as you try to introduce new thinking into your organization, but it is even worse when in addition to getting stalled, you are also shunned for being "difficult" or "pushy." If you cannot change the thought process in your organization or your department within a year, do you really want to invest a second year beating your head against the wall?

9. The danger of working in a slow-moving, boxy environment is that it will turn you into a pod person yourself. You will stop having great ideas and start to be content with the status quo. You will tell yourself, "At least I have a stable job and a good salary. What else do I need?"

10. When you get beat up enough for daring to suggest new ideas, you will stop speaking up. You will keep your ideas to yourself. Who benefits then? Your customers don't benefit. Your shareholders don't benefit. You can make

yourself sick by pretending that your job is fine when in fact it is killing your spirit.

2016 is half over. The calendar is advancing -- is your career advancing too? Is your flame growing at work, or is it shrinking? You deserve to work in a place where the people are smart and unafraid of new ideas.

You deserve a job where your talents are celebrated and where you can bring yourself to work every day. It doesn't cost anything to check out the job market. That's a step you can take by yourself. You don't need anyone's permission but your own!

HOW TO FIND WORK YOU LOVE --
AND WHY MOST PEOPLE DON'T TRY

When kids are very little, we tell them "Be whoever you want to be!" but as kids get older, the message changes.

By the time most kids are in middle school, the adults around them have begun teaching them to be practical. Little by little kids stop believing that their grandest dreams can come true.

Some kids grow up without losing their faith in themselves — or their belief that they can accomplish whatever they want to accomplish and become whoever they want to be. What's different about those kids?

Maybe the kids who hang onto their dreams have support from their family members, who tell them not to give up on their most audacious plans.

Maybe they faced adversity early on and overcame it, learning in the process that most of the obstacles we face are not as formidable as we have been led to believe they are.

Maybe the kids who never give up on their dreams are kids who just don't care what other people think. It takes guts to depart from the standard path: Go to school, get good grades, find a good job and keep it whether you like the job, or not.

It takes courage to say, "I want to make my own path!"

At any working age it is possible to move closer to your dreams, find work that celebrates you, and run your career like the business it is.

Your career is a business just as surely as any multinational corporation is. It is your ship to steer — but only if you know how much power you possess!

The first step in finding work that will ask more of you — making use of your talents, personality and passion — and also give you back more than a paycheck is to give yourself permission to dream again.

As adults we can feel foolish or exposed when we allow ourselves to dream really big -- the way we used to do when we were kids. But without a big dream to follow, how could anyone take the big steps that will move them into the life and career they want?

The first step is to give yourself permission to create a vision for your life and career.

I'm not talking about setting goals — that comes much later. In the absence of a vision for your life, goals are nothing more than items on your to-do list. To find work you love, you have to get outside your comfort zone and create a vision for your life and career.

Here's how to do it:

1. Get a journal and start writing in it. Write about what you want in your life and career. Don't censor yourself. If you want to act in the movies, write it down. Many famous actors started acting later in their lives. If you want to run a business, explore your creative side, have more money or change your location - write it down!

2. Accept and embrace the fact that everything that has happened in your life so far was meant to happen just as it did. When we complain about our circumstances (stupid job, bad boss, etc.) and look at our current situation as hopeless, embarrassing or less than we deserve, we create our own obstacles to success. Successful people can say "I don't like my life right now. Oh well - that's okay. I'm not a victim of it. I can change it. Everything happens for a reason. Maybe the hardships I've experienced needed to

happen so that I could finally focus on changing my life for the better."

3. Spell out your vision for your life in as much detail as you can. "One day I want to work on Wall Street" is not a vision. Get very granular. I tell my students to picture the clothes they'll be wearing when they walk onstage to accept the award they earned for whatever great achievement they have in mind. Picture the auditorium, the audience and the person who presents you with the award. The more clearly you see your own future, the easier it will be for you to steer in the direction you want.

4. Recognize that the reason most of us don't shoot for our dreams is that it's scary to do so. We may have people around us saying "Who do you think you are? You're no one special. Who are you to have big dreams?" Those people don't deserve to be part of your vision. Don't tell anyone about your plans except for people who support you in your quest. You might decide to tell no one about your vision, and that's fine.

5. As your vision takes shape, look at its place in your life from altitude — that is, with perspective. The first response our fearful brains serve up when we create a grand vision is "That vision is impractical! It would take you years to reach it!" So what? That's all we have — years. We have time, or at least we hope to. What else would we do with our time apart from working toward our vision? Get up above your day-to-day struggles and see your path going back to your birth and stretching out to the horizon. Once you see it, you can take your path wherever you want it to go!

6. Now, put together a plan to move into the career and life you want. Lay out the steps. Some of them will be short-term objectives. Some will take longer. Here's an example to guide you.

Monica is a medical office director. She makes good money (and she doesn't have a bachelor's degree) but she's not happy in her job. Her physicians are impatient and unappreciative, and she doesn't like the way her practice treats its patients.

Monica realizes over time that she's wasting her gifts keeping her medical practice running smoothly. For a few years she's been hoping that someone or something would swoop in and save her.

Gradually it dawns on Monica that if anyone is going to save her, it's going to be Monica herself.

Monica gives herself permission to dream big, the way she did when she was little.

When she was a kid Monica was crazy about horses. She didn't love horseback riding lessons, but she loved hanging around with horses. Monica could see that horses held a special place in her heart.

She would love to work with horses as a job, somehow — but how?

"What possible qualifications do I have to work with horses?" Monica's fearful brain asked her.

"Pipe down," Monica told her brain. "The key is to take a step in the direction of my dream, rather than dismissing it as foolish."

Monica started researching organizations related to horses.

She was amazed how many organizations she found.

Monica took a step and joined the Board of Directors of a not-for-profit agency that raised money to buy wild mustangs that had been rounded up and removed from their habitat and found them new homes with loving caretakers.

Monica had never been on a not-for-profit Board before. She was almost silent at the first few Board meetings, but gradually her confidence grew.

Monica was shocked to see how just being a Board member reignited her passion for horses.

She decided to finish her bachelor's degree, emphasizing finance and fund-raising. By the time Monica graduated from night school two years later, she was president of the Board of Directors and had helped to raise over $150,000 to find homes for mustangs.

In her volunteer work Monica felt strong and capable. As president of the Board Monica talked to local CEOs almost every day. "My day job sucks my energy away," Monica realized, "but my unpaid night job builds my energy up!"

Four months after walking across the stage to accept her diploma, Monica accepted a job as Executive Director for a new not-for-profit organization devoted to advocacy for wild mustangs. Monica helped to found the organization and when the Board launched its search for an E.D., they say "Monica, you are the obvious choice!"

Monica started her new job on her 51st birthday, but her journey had begun the day she realized she was miserable in her medical practice job, three years earlier.

You can do the same thing Monica did. You can step through the fear that keeps most people stuck in unhappy work situations. You can give yourself permission to dream again, the way you did when you were tiny.

It's your life. No one else gets to decide how you invest your time and talents. You are steering the ship — but only if you know how much power you have!

TEN REASONS GOOD EMPLOYEES GET FIRED

For years we were taught — and most of us believed — that working hard and hitting your goals at work would practically guarantee career success.

Now we know better.

Now we know that the most important thing in any organization is not the company's strategy, its products and services or its stock price.

These are all outcomes. The most important thing in any organization is the quality of the energy flowing from top to bottom and across and throughout the place.

The most important thing in any organization is the culture.

Every company, government agency and not-for-profit is an organism, and they all function the way any organism does. When the organism is healthy, good things happen.

When the organism is unhealthy, nothing good happens. Movement is slow and sluggish. You can tell when a company culture goes bad -- because culture is the loudest thing happening in any workplace.

The health of the organism you work for is incredibly important to you, no matter what your job description is.

Many a smart and talented working person has learned this lesson the hard way. They met their goals, pleased their customers and gave every ounce of their talent and commitment to the job — but they still ran into trouble.

Maybe they upset someone higher up the food chain by being too good at their job or speaking more truth than the senior leadership team was ready to hear.

They didn't make any mistakes except one: they missed the signs that their organization/organism was unhealthy enough to cast them out simply for calling attention to the bad energy swirling around.

You might not even have to name the toxic energy swirling around you to upset the powers that be.

You might keep quiet about it and still make people angry, because people in fear are good at reading energy. They are vigilant. They are so afraid that they can easily see you as their enemy, even when you sincerely want to help.

Here are ten reasons capable and talented people get fired:

Ten Reasons Good Employees Get Fired

1. You can get fired if your excellent results on the job cause embarrassment to higher-level managers. They may think that you must be cutting corners to hit your goals so easily. They would rather get rid of you than ask "How did you do it? We'd like you to teach everyone else to do what you're doing."

2. You can get fired for asking questions no one wants to answer or even think about — questions like "Are we sure this is still the best way to handle this process?" or "What is the long-term plan?"

3. You can get fired for setting normal boundaries like "I will finish that project on Monday rather than take it home over the weekend" or "I'm sorry, I can't tell the Executive Team that everything is fine with the production schedule, because it's not."

4. You can get fired for naming the elephant in the room — the topic that desperately needs airtime but isn't getting it.

5. You can get fired for having a better idea than your boss's idea.

6. You can get fired for getting too much positive attention from top leaders in your organization. Some fearful managers are like amoebae. They operate like single-celled creatures. They don't make fine distinctions; they see everyone in their sphere as either predator or prey. If you look like a predator to them, they will get rid of you in a heartbeat. You might look like a predator to your fearful boss if higher-up managers are paying too much attention to you!

7. You can get fired for doing such a good job that other departments get angry. Other managers may tell your supervisor "Your employee is showing off and making us look bad!"

8. You can get fired for having too much visibility outside your company — being asked to speak at events, getting awards or having an article published. If you work in an unhealthy organism, they will not appreciate your public affirmation!

9. You can get fired for moving too fast and having too many ideas for your managers' taste. A fearful amoeba manager can easily feel threatened — and might toss you out rather than suffer the indignity of having to listen to a subordinate.

10. You can get fired for accomplishing so much at work that your boss wonders "Will this employee come after my job next?"

There is nothing dishonorable about getting fired. It happens to outstanding employees all the time. If it happens to you, remember that not every manager — or every employer — deserves your talents. Only the people who get you, deserve you!

People send me job ads every day. They know that I love to read jobs, which say so much about an employer's culture and values. Job ads in general are pretty sad, and some of the saddest ones I see are the ads for HR leaders. They say things like "HR VP needed – strong comp skills." What do we know, so far? We know that we're talking about a company that puts knowledge of compensation schemes at the top of its priority list for the chief people officer. We are talking about the person who will lead the cultural charge for this employer, the person who'll go out and grab the talent our customers need us to have and our competitors want to get themselves. Here is the person who will debate with the CEO and the executive team to make sure the organization is doing the right thing by its employees, the people who create value for shareholders. And here's a company that really, really wants an HR VP who understands the details of compensation plan mechanics, above all.

That's a bad sign.

If you were an employee working for that company, you'd be wise to be very nervous reading that HR-VP job ad. The ad tells you exactly how your employer feels about the HR function, and by extension, how your employer feels about you.

Would we hire a Marketing VP because he or she is an expert in marketing software? I hope not. I hope we'd look for a Marketing VP with vision and fortitude, someone who can spot what isn't obvious in the competitive landscape and start fertile conversations with the people around him or her on important topics, every day. I hope your Marketing VP is a visionary person, and I hope your HR VP is one, too.

Many HR VPs are not that. They are capable administrators. Under their watch, the EEO-1 forms get filed on time, and the insurance premiums get paid. Your organization needs much more than that in an HR leader, if it wants to compete in the global, diverse, virtual and connected world of business.

I spoke at an HR conference last week, and afterward a woman told me that when she worked in for several years at one HR job, her boss was the most-feared manager in the company. "People would poke their heads into the HR department," she told me, "and cock their heads over to one side, asking us silently in sign language 'Is Gail in?' If Gail, the scary HR VP, were in her office, people wouldn't come into the department.

When Gail was somewhere else, they'd come in and talk to us." That's not what you want in an HR leader. The person running the people function should be approachable by any employee – and should seek out those relationships, avidly. How do you function as a cheerleader for talent and performance when people are afraid to talk to you?

How do you create pipelines that allow great ideas to reach the executive suite and that highlight talent anywhere in the ranks if you're viewed as fearsome and bureaucratic? Here's the answer: you don't. The era of the overbearing, fussy, officious HR biddy is over. Here's our list of ten must-have elements every CEO should demand in an HR chief. How does your HR leader rate?

BUSINESS INSTINCT.

Your HR chief is the person most responsible for keeping your talent engine fueled and running, and talent is your company's biggest expense. That means your HR VP needs a solid business mind – not just an understanding of how business works and how money is made, but enough curiosity about the business to continue asking questions, keep learning, and make business education a fundamental feature of your company's culture. If you're the CEO, ask yourself:

- Could your HR VP sit on a panel tomorrow and represent your business faithfully to attendees who don't know your company's story?

- Could your HR chief identify right now the three strategic priorities for your business next year, and why they matter, and how you're primed to reach them – not a recitation of what's in the written plan, but with an understanding of exactly what's needed to hit each goal, and why?

- Does your HR leader have strong relationships in the business community, and your Board of Directors' numbers on his or her speed dial?

- Does your HR executive see his or her role in building the organization? Is he or she someone who takes personal responsibility for making the team the greatest competitive advantage your company has - or someone who comes to work each day to prevent disaster in the form of a violated policy or an employee-relations incident?

LISTENING.

The HR leader in your company has to understand what's happening on the ground. An HR chief who sits in an office with the door closed is not going to make your company a great place to work or a great vendor to its customers. Your chief people officer must be easy to talk to. He or she has to be someone who wants to know what's happening with the troops, in the business and among its customers. Your HR leader should be at your Sales-team offsite meetings and every major company gathering, and should know your customers, too. How else could s/he build a customer-focused team? If you're the CEO, ask yourself:

- Is your HR leader a great listener? Is he or she available to the troops, and a mentor to employees inside and outside HR?

- Does your HR chief have an ear to the ground all the time, strong contacts throughout the organization, and influence with people in the boardroom and on the loading dock?

- Is your HR chief available to employees throughout the company and to the HR staff? Is s/he reachable, accessible, and compassionate? Is s/he worthy of confidences, and the soul of discretion? Do employees believe that what they've shared with the HR VP will stay confidential?

CHAMPION FOR TALENT.

In the simplest model for HR leadership, there are two distinct kinds of HR officers. One of them is champion for talent, always spotting and exalting great people. The other one is a zealot for rules and regulations, always making sure that the employees don't sue the company. You want the first kind. If you're the CEO, ask yourself:

- Does your HR VP talk about talent, performance, and culture all day long? Does he or she have an eye for up-and-coming people, and does s/he take time to mentor and reinforce young and older employees in their goals and aspirations?

- Does your HR chief advocate for the people in your company, making introductions and proposing learning experiences on the fly? Does he or she view the growth of leaders in your organization as a principal, personal goal?

- Will your HR officer go to bat for employees, when it's inconvenient or expensive – but essential -- to do the right thing for the sake of your employer brand and culture?

CONSIGLIERE.

In the consigliere pantheon, no one can touch Robert Duvall's character in "The Godfather," Tom Hagen. Tom advised Vito Corleone and later, his son Michael, advising them on the many complicated staff issues involved in running a large and sprawling organized-crime family riddled with entanglements and risks, not to mention bullets and prison sentences. Of course, most of us aren't advising Mafia dons, so our jobs may be slightly easier (and less personally risky) than Tom Hagen's job was, but the role is the same. An HR chief serves as eyes and ears for the CEO – not in a "Big Brother is watching" way but in the sense of someone who knows what is going on in the ranks, has the trust of the employees and can tell the CEO what s/he doesn't want to hear (but needs to). If you're the CEO, ask yourself:

- Does your HR chief often shift your thinking about individual leadership situations or your company culture as a whole? Does he or she regularly shake you out of your frame as a leader?

- Part of the senior HR role is to challenge the status quo. On a scale of zero (never steps outside the box) to always (your HR exec is the chief provocateur in the joint), how well does your HR VP re-focus leadership thinking to keep it in synch with reality?

- Do the VPs of other functions, and your business-unit presidents if you've got any, view your HR leader as a credible and wise advisor to them in their leadership roles?

COMMUNICATOR.

Apart from talent championship, another fundamental role for an HR leader is internal communication. It's fine to send out benefits surveys and policy manual updates, but those things are administrative bulletins, not cultural communication. Your HR chief needs to be able to design and deliver communication whose purpose is to enliven the troops and keep people well-informed and motivated. Your HR leader should be a communications strategist, always looking for clever ways to engage the team and keep them in the loop with the firm's plans, triumphs and opportunities. If you're the CEO, ask yourself:

- Is your HR chief a strong, inspiring and empathetic communicator? Does he or she take on the role of keeping people informed about the company, its competitors, upcoming activities and challenges?

- Does your HR function emphasize internal communications, including discussion of audiences, communication goals, messages and channels? Does your HR leader understand the relationship between important company initiatives (a new sales system, or a strategic re-organization), the communication of those plans, and team buy-in? Is top-drawer communication built into every bullet on the HR strategic plan, and is two-way communication (top-down broadcast-type outreach and bottom-up feedback, not just the CYA employee engagement survey but multiple, grassroots 'listening' mechanisms) baked into your HR strategy?

OPPORTUNIST.

You can write an HR strategic plan, and I hope you do. After the ink is dry on the page, new circumstances will arise. A strong HR leader is nimble. He or she can deal with changing circumstances and jump on opportunities as they present themselves. A ready-for-prime-time HR chief has rock-solid relationships with people throughout your organization (and outside its walls) that will get your HR chief quickly into the middle of conversations about building your talent pool, pulling in new capabilities through strategic alliances, or taking a great idea generated down in the guts of your organization and elevating it. If you're the CEO, ask yourself:

- Is my HR chief well-connected enough to hear about opportunities for breakthroughs as they happen – a process used in one group that's replicable elsewhere in the organization, or a marketing push in one group that could benefit from the participation of another – and well-trusted enough to be the conduit and broker for those opportunities?

- Is my HR leader someone who spots the junctures where brilliant ideas can flourish – and is s/he influential enough to champion those initiatives, once spotted?

ROLE MODEL.

It's hard to work in any organization, and large organizations are especially tricky. In a large organization, you've got multiple personalities to deal with, competing priorities, lots of formal structure, and the complications and irritations that come into play whenever large numbers of people try to coordinate their activities. An HR leader sets the cultural tone, and through his or her actions sends the message "Great ideas can thrive here." Your HR chief is a role model for other managers, and for employees in general. He or she has to be a truth-teller, a non-bureaucrat and a minister for healthy culture. You will not thrive with an HR leader who is fearful, political, an information-hoarder or a toady. If you're the CEO, ask yourself:

- Is my HR chief one of the ablest leaders in our company?

- Does my HR leader do the things I ask leaders to do – hire people smarter that s/he is, give credit to the team, mentor up-and-coming leaders and give thoughtful, honest feedback? Does s/he handle conflict in a forthright and human-centered way, or embroil the HR department in political wrangles with other groups?

- Could my HR chief teach a leadership course to his or her fellow managers today (and if s/he did, would anyone come)?

- Does my HR leader invite opinions about how the HR function (and he or she personally) could be stronger in championing talent in our company?

STRATEGIST.

A CEO boss of mine once said "Strategy is easy. Execution is hard." Another name for the execution of strategy in people-filled organizations is "HR strategy." Once the business knows where it's headed competitively and what constitutes a win, your HR chief has to pull the groups together to make the strategy come to life. An HR chief whose annual strategic plan revolves around reducing dental-plan premiums and evaluating the overtime policy is not someone who can help you stride forward to win in the global economy. If you're the CEO, ask yourself:

- Is my HR chief a strategic guru? Does s/he add valuable input to conversations about our topmost business strategy, and take on the execution of our strategic plans as a personal mission (through leadership communication, rewards, team-building, the definition of roles and goals, and in 'soft' ways) every day?

- Do my HR leader's briefings at staff meetings focus on issues that are central to our success in the marketplace, or on administrative and tactical HR-department topics?

- If you asked your HR leader today, "If I told you to go get the top 100 people in any industry who could grow our business fifty percent faster than the growth target in our plan, and to have them here in ninety days ready to go, how would you do it?" what would s/he say? If the answer is heavy on process and protestations about recent HR staff cuts and the crushing workload in HR already, you've got your work cut out for you.

EVANGELIST.

Your company's culture and its story are your power. You can't create any financial, technical or marketing advantage that will keep you safe from competitive attacks. Those advantages are fleeting. You can build organizational capability to withstand those attacks if you focus on building a healthy and winning culture. If you take the time and make the investment to build an engine for innovation and great ideas, your competitors will have a hard time keeping up with you. Your HR person is the minister of that culture, the person most responsible for keeping the cultural pixie dust flying around the building and reinforcing your team. If your HR person isn't a cheerleader for your brand, then who will be? If you're the CEO, ask yourself:

- Is your HR VP someone who sees opportunities for strengthening the culture in every conversation and email message? Is his or her focus on the human transactions that

HR requires (payroll changes, vacation requests, and the like) or on the transformational aspects of the job, including reinforcement of the company culture and constant acknowledgement of the demands we're making on the team?

- Could you send your HR VP to a meeting of unhappy employees today with the expectation that s/he would go with open ears, hear the issues, discuss them forthrightly and non-defensively, and leave the audience feeling better than when they arrived about the company and its values?

- Do your employees tell you "I met with Marjorie, the HR VP, and I could tell she really cared about what I was telling her?" or do they get put off and talked down to? Does your attorney tell you that your organization has an unusually low (or high) incidence of employment-law matters for a company your size?

SALESPERSON.

My dad, a retired business-magazine publisher, used to tell me "Everyone is in sales." I'd say "Dad, I'm not in sales – I'm an HR person." Of course, my dad was right. We are all in sales. We have to sell our ideas, for starters. HR people sell a lot more than ideas – they sell the company as a prospective employer to job candidates, and they re-sell the company as an employer to their employees every day. If you're the CEO, ask yourself:

- What major initiatives did my HR chief sell me and my executive team on, in the last six months? How well did he or she sell those ideas?

- Can my HR leader sell top-level job candidates on our opportunities? If a prospective CFO were talking with three employers at once and I sent my HR chief to meet the CFO candidate in the CFO's home city, would my HR person come back with a signed offer letter?

- Can my HR leader sell his or her ideas internally, before getting my support? Does my HR chief know how to read people, to overcome objections, to build support for ideas and to shift his or her thinking to incorporate other people's priorities?

HR leadership isn't easy. It isn't for the faint of heart. It can't resemble the old-fashioned process-heavy HR leadership role, not if we want our organizations to flourish. One HR headhunter I know tells me that only fifteen percent of the HR execs she encounters are ready for HR senior leadership in a talent-hungry world. If eighty-five percent of HR chiefs in the ecosystem are behind the curve, don't get stuck with one of them leading the charge for talent in your shop. Use our checklist to make sure you're one of the lucky CEOs with a make-it-happen HR chief at his or her side; then, rejoice.

BECAUSE EMPLOYEES CAN'T BE TRUSTED

Because employees can't be trusted, we have put in place a massive system of policies and controls to make sure no one steps out of line. It costs hundreds of millions of shareholder and customer dollars to manage this system, but it must be worth it because we're so certain our employees are untrustworthy—notwithstanding the fact that we hired every one of them ourselves.

We run people through online honesty tests, writing tests, background checks, and drug tests, but we must have hard evidence that employees still can't be trusted. If we didn't have that evidence, why would we subject every one of our employees to soul-crushing, forced-ranking exercises and constant performance appraisals? If our leadership behavior is any guide, our employees are not to be trusted—not for a femtosecond.

Because employees can't be trusted, we put in place policies that require our co-workers to bring in evidence of a doctor's visit when they are sick, no matter how much they tell us they hate to be out because of the stress it will cause them when they return, and no matter that half the city is down with the same virus. Since employees can't be relied upon, we require them to bring in a funeral notice proving that Aunt Sally really died last week—no matter that everyone in the department has met Aunt Sally at social gatherings, or that we consoled our co-worker during Aunt Sally's protracted illness.

Policies such as the proof-of-death protocol are expensive to administer, so it must be beyond doubt that our employees—whatever our relationships day-to-day with them may be—are unworthy of our trust.

Since employees are conniving little beggars likely to shank us the moment our backs our turned, we hold them to weekly, monthly, and quarterly milestones. If we were to trust them to carry out a project without close supervision, who knows what wrong step they might take? Our job ads require applicants to have 15 years of experience, suggesting that the people we bring into our shops might have passed all the can-you-be-trusted tests in our collective corporate quivers many jobs ago. Fifteen years is a long time, but we can't be too careful. Even a 15-year veteran can breach a policy or make a misstep, and the ramifications of that could be horrible. (Say, the wrong typeface ends up in a product brochure, requiring reprinting at a cost of $400.)

Our leadership systems scream: "We love our customers. Our employees? Different story."

If we were to treat our customers the way we treat employees, they'd run for the hills. Somehow, because customers give us their cash, we believe their every wish is our command. Since employees give us only their brains, guts, emotional connection, time, and goodwill, the deal is slightly different. We treat our employees as though they're only waiting for the chance to take us down.

We write mistrust into our management guidelines. We institutionalize it in our policy handbooks. We reinforce it with every insulting memo and "to the staff" broadcast e-mail. We ding employees when they forget their ID badges and penalize them for leaving work a half-hour early to pay a traffic ticket. We willingly take and make the most of the juice and spark our teammates bring us because they can't help connecting to their work at a level far above what the paycheck requires, but we fall back down to the level of the transaction as soon as it's convenient to do so.

When it matters, we say: "It's business." When we need the extra effort, the last mile, the work-all-weekend push, or the thankless, endless trip to God-knows-where, then it's all about the team. We don't deserve the trust we get in those moments, but humans are trusting.

If we value talent, we'll start dismantling the lumbering Godzilla of controls and policies that hampers creativity in virtually every organization, and we'll start trusting ourselves to hire people we trust. Then our jobs will get easier and the energy at work will improve dramatically. What are we waiting for?

THE QUESTION EVERY CEO SHOULD ASK THE COMPANY'S HR LEADER

What do CEOs and their HR chiefs talk about? With luck, they talk about everything -- about hiring, and the state of the organization, and upcoming events. I hope they talk about who's getting promoted and who's leaving and what's new and how the team is holding up.

There's one question every CEO should ask his or her HR leader every time they meet, and that question is "Do our employees love working here?"

That is an easy question to answer. The HR VP can say "Not enough of them do, honestly," and then s/he and the CEO can talk about how to improve the culture in the organization.

The HR VP can say "They love it here, and I'm working directly with the few people who don't love it -- some of whom are not a great fit for us, and the rest of whom have pointed out issues that we really need to fix, and that we're going to fix this quarter."

Those are the only possible answers. If the answer would be "No, people don't love working here" then it's highly unlikely that the CEO would have asked the question in the first place.

In the business world and other workplaces, we are re-orienting ourselves to the idea that every one of our employees is a volunteer. Sure, we pay them a salary, but any organization would pay them the same salary.

We're not going to get people excited just by paying them a salary that they deserve in the talent market anyway. We have to assume that our employees could work anywhere, but they chose to work with us. We have to honor that choice every day.

Employee Engagement Surveys are an expensive and insulting waste of time. Anyone with two functioning brain cells can see through the Employee Engagement Survey, a sad CYA exercise that doesn't get at the heart of the question "Do you love your job?"

An HR person should ask that question fifty times a day. S/he can say "It's my job to make your job easier and more fun. What do you need from me?"

When people ask me "What is your view on the changing work ethic?" I say "An employee's job is to give his or her best at work every day. A manager's job is to give the employee a reason to come back to work tomorrow."

We have to make the goal "Our company will be an amazing place to work" our highest goal -- higher than our sales-growth goal or any other financial metric. If we don't do that, how could we expect our employees to work as hard and as passionately as our customer-satisfaction goals and our financial goals will require them to work?

We have to work every day to make our organizations amazing places to work. What does that mean, exactly?

1. It means that we listen to our employees whether they're sharing ideas with us or letting us know how we screwed up. We don't turn them off just because we don't want to hear what they have to say.

2. It means that we tell our employees how big a contribution they make to the company's success. The team of people we work with is responsible for 100% of the good things that happen for us. They deserve 100% of the credit. If we're stingy with praise, we don't deserve our people. If managers keep the credit for themselves, they don't deserve to represent our brands.

3. It means that we talk openly about fear and trust, and about blockages in the energy that deplete our Team Energy and keep people stressed and unhappy. It doesn't matter what sort of blockage we're dealing with -- bureaucratic red tape, political struggles, out-of-date systems or a VP who shouldn't have the position that s/he does --- we have to talk about it. The stickier the topic is, the more it needs to be aired and resolved.

4. It means that we treat our employees like valued collaborators rather than cogs in our machine. We value their personal lives outside of work. We talk with them as humans rather than measuring everything they do and holding them up to countless yardsticks.

5. Lastly, it means that we are always asking "What can we do better?" and taking the advice we get.

We don't think twice about delighting our customers and overwhelming them with outstanding service and attention to their needs. Why would we treat our employees any differently?

DO WE STILL NEED HUMAN RESOURCES?

When I was twenty-four, I managed an Order Processing department for a greeting card company on the north side of Chicago. I loved my job. We had a great crew and we got a ton of work done.

I was finishing my degree on the weekends and singing a lot. I wasn't thinking about changing jobs. My boss, John Brady, asked me to travel an hour south to our distribution center and help the employees there sort out some issues they were having working with the main office in Chicago. I did. I set up meetings and listened to the issues, and helped get them handled.

Later that summer, I was on vacation with my sister in Martha's Vineyard. I was twenty-four and my sister was twenty-seven. I flew to Boston and the two of us went to Martha's Vineyard and had a great time. We went to clubs at night and went to the beach and drove around the island by day. On the last day of our vacation I called our office to check in. My colleague Louise said, "There's a rumor that you're not our boss anymore."

"Can you please transfer me to John Brady's line?" I asked her.

John said "Somehow the message got out ahead of time and I apologize for that. I'm switching your job. You're going to be our HR Manager."

I was dumbstruck. I loved working with my team, with our customers and our sales reps. I liked the fast pace of my job. When there was a greeting card store opening somewhere in the country and fixtures were being shipped from all over, it was fun to help orchestrate the action. I couldn't imagine how I could have fun in HR. All I knew of HR was deadly boring pronouncements and policies. My voice shook on the phone as I talked with John. I felt betrayed, because I had worked so hard.

"You're going to like it, Liz," said John.

I moved into HR. I knew that there were laws and regulations I had to learn about. I went to seminars and workshops nearly every week. The rest of the time my door was open. I talked to our employees in the office, in the field and down in the distribution center. I was swamped with visits and inquiries. I saw immediately what the job of HR is: to take care of the team's morale and to build Team Energy. The job of HR is to keep the energy moving and to make an organization the best place to work that it can be.

At the workshops and seminars, I attended outside our office, there was very little talk about motivation and morale. We talked about sick day allowances and laws concerning overtime. I couldn't see why there was such a focus on laws. If you treat people decently, you're not going to break many laws. When we deal with our customers, we don't say "Our focus here is to obey the laws with respect to serving our customers."

The laws about customer-vendor relationships are set at a very low bar. If you're breaking a law in your dealings with customers, you're not going to have very many customers anyway. Most of us set our sales and customer-service standards much higher than what the law requires.

Somehow our outlook is different when it comes to employees. We put employment laws on a pedestal instead of seeing them as table stakes – the absolute minimum requirements. Of course, we have to comply with employment laws, but that goes without saying. We don't mistreat or defraud our customers if we can help it and hopefully we feel at least as warmly toward our own coworkers.

The job of HR is to become an organization's Ministry of Culture, celebrating and reinforcing the awesomeness of the people who work there. I had a blast in that job. Then one of our employees got sick.

AIDS was brand new in Chicago in the early eighties. Our employees were a diverse group. Our company was situated in the middle of the hipster lakefront neighborhood. We hired everyone - punk rockers and downtown-type businesspeople and young gay folks coming in from all over the country to live in a city where they could be themselves.

There was a Gay Pride parade back then, but our gay employees still got treated roughly by the police and more than once, an employee of ours was arrested just for walking down the street in drag.

Reality hit us in the face when our employee Jack, our beloved, brilliant and funny IT manager, got sick and died of AIDs. Jack was diagnosed about a week before he died.

We were in shock, and then other men started getting sick. I called the HR association for help.

"What do I do?" I asked them. I was sure there were handbooks and posters and advice to be shared. There was nothing.

"I have guys in my office crying, because their boyfriends are dying and they may die themselves," I said.

I was twenty-four. AIDs was not an HR topic at that time. Death was not an HR topic. There was no policy involved in it, so it didn't exist.

Twenty men in our company got sick. The real job of HR was ignored while we talked at HR events about timesheets and the new field of HRIS and dress code policies. The focus was all wrong. "We are talking about the wrong things," I thought, and said out loud often enough that I got a reputation. "Our job is about people!"

We don't need mechanical, quantitative HR in our companies. Any organization that hasn't outsourced the spreadsheet half of HR is wasting its precious resources, money and time. The real job of HR is down on the ground and out on the street with the team members. Our job is to listen and advise. Our job is to talk and act to make our organization an amazing, vibrant, human place to work.

That's the only job of HR. The clerical and administrative stuff is necessary but not nearly sufficient. If your organization is still treating HR like a compliance function, you're missing the power that is available to you when you hire human beings to work on your team. An HR function without a beating human heart is worse than unnecessary. It's a drag on your ability to do whatever you're trying to do. You need an HR function, and you need people in it who are out with the employees listening and building community.

Your HR folks spread pixie dust around, and they tell you when your pixie dust dispenser is getting low. They tell you the truth about what's working and not working in the organization. That's the real job of HR.

We still need HR. We need it more than ever now. We need to bring the human back into work in a big way. We need to develop Ministries of Culture in every organization. It's a shift in perspective and it starts when you find your voice as an HR person. There are more and more Ministers of Culture stepping into their power every day. Join us!

If you'd like to join the Human Workplace™ movement to reinvent work for people (and get tons of free resources & inspiration for your HR mission) please visit this URL:

Humanworkplace.com/redbloodedHR